Speed Reading for Better Grades

by

Ward Cramer

illustrated by Mike Gorman

J. WESTON
WALCH
PUBLISHER
Portland, Maine

User's Guide
to
Walch Reproducible Books

As part of our general effort to provide educational materials that are as practical and economical as possible, we have designated this publication a "reproducible book." The designation means that the purchase of the book includes purchase of the right to limited reproduction of all pages on which this symbol appears:

Here is the basic Walch policy: We grant to individual purchasers of this book the right to make sufficient copies of reproducible pages for use by all students of a single teacher. This permission is limited to a single teacher and does not apply to entire schools or school systems, so institutions purchasing the book should pass the permission on to a single teacher. Copying of the book or its parts for resale is prohibited.

Any questions regarding this policy or request to purchase further reproduction rights should be addressed to:

Permissions Editor
J. Weston Walch, Publisher
321 Valley Street • P.O. Box 658
Portland, Maine 04104-0658

1   2   3   4   5   6   7   8   9   1 0

ISBN 0-8250-3803-5

Copyright © 1978, 1998
J. Weston Walch, Publisher
P. O. Box 658 • Portland, Maine 04104-0658
Printed in the United States of America

Contents

INTRODUCTION   *v*

WHAT DOES RESEARCH SAY ABOUT SPEED READING?   *vii*

WHAT YOU SHOULD KNOW ABOUT READING
   —STUDENT INVENTORY   *ix*

TO THE TEACHER   *xiii*

Lesson 1   WHAT IS AN EFFICIENT READER?   1

Lesson 2   COMMON READING FAULTS   9

Lesson 3   EYE MOVEMENTS   17

Lesson 4   BUILD YOUR VOCABULARY   25

Lesson 5   READING PURPOSE IS THE KEY TO COMPREHENSION   33

Lesson 6   PREVIEWING   41

Lesson 7   READ IN THOUGHT UNITS   49

Lesson 8   SKIMMING AND SCANNING   57

Lesson 9   SKIMMING FOR THE MAIN IDEA   65

Lesson 10   SKIMMING FOR DETAILS   73

Lesson 11   IMPROVE YOUR SPEED IN SOCIAL STUDIES   81

Lesson 12   IMPROVE YOUR SPEED IN MATHEMATICS   89

Lesson 13   IMPROVE YOUR SPEED IN SCIENCE   97

Lesson 14   IMPROVE YOUR SPEED IN LITERATURE   105

Lesson 15   STUDY-READING AND MEMORY   113

Lesson 16   CONTINUING PROGRESS THROUGH PRACTICE   121

APPENDIX   *129*

ANSWERS   *135*

Introduction

This revised edition includes new, updated reading selections, a new lesson, "Improve Your Speed in Literature," and added sections such as "What Does Research Say About Speed Reading?" and "What You Should Know About Reading—A Student Inventory." The emphasis is still on helping students improve their reading skills in both speed and comprehension. *Speed Reading for Better Grades* can be used as a three-week concentrated course or as a sporadic course of study. This book can also be used effectively in conjunction with language arts or social studies classes.

Most students have the ability to read all types of material much faster than they do now, but few take the time or make the effort to improve these vital skills. Most people read too slowly for their own benefit, laboring under the impression that to understand and retain factual information, reading must be done slowly. This is a false assumption. By increasing reading speed and concentrating upon what is read, more material is covered and retention of what's been read is greater. Increasing speed, however, without an accompanying increase in comprehension doesn't solve anything. The two must go together.

This speed reading course is designed to help students train themselves to read faster and retain more of what they read. No matter how fast or slow their present rate, it can be improved. This fact has been proven by tens of thousands of junior and senior high school students who have used this same material and have doubled their reading speed and comprehension.

These pages contain no magic formulas or hocus-pocus rituals. Their content is based upon one of the easiest, quickest, and most practical methods known, providing a series of discussions on reading problems, skills, and techniques, a series of timed skill-building exercises, and reading passages with tests of comprehension.

One of the most important elements in improving reading speed is that of discipline or self-control. Students must recognize that improvement does not take place overnight, although at the conclusion of the course they should see observable improvement in both speed and comprehension. One reason so many self-improvement programs fail is simply because there is so little self-discipline. This is the purpose for the teacher's supervision. Without external motivation, most students soon give up.

Another important phase of a speed reading course is the attitude with which the student enters the program. Repetition in itself does not improve reading rate or comprehension. This means that the student must make a real effort to improve with each lesson. Each lesson must be a challenge. If students simply read the exercises without really trying, there is no point in beginning the program.

Another thing: It is going to take more than simply doing the exercises in class. Students must practice what they learn during homework and in all reading activities. Ask students to do as much easy reading at home as time will allow while the course is in session (an hour per day would be appropriate). All practice helps. They shouldn't begin free-time practice with textbooks! Studying a textbook usually doesn't improve speed or comprehension in the early stages of any program. Ask students to take it easy, read fun books, books they will enjoy, books they have always wanted to read but couldn't find the time to read. Later on, students will graduate to more difficult material as speed improves. Remember, difficult material is read more slowly than easy material, but reading speed on both types will be measurably increased after completing this course. A formula for determining the grade level of reading materials is found on page xiii of "To the Teacher." It is fairly accurate and provides a basis for beginning with easy material before graduating to more difficult or higher grade level materials.

And for students' encouragement, there is a series of charts in the back of the book in which students may plot their progress through all the exercises and stories as they complete their work. Ask students to plot a line graph and watch their improvement. Each student is competing against himself or herself, not someone else in the class.

The *interpretation* exercises are prepared to help students develop an ability to "think" as they read. Regardless of how efficiently students use their eyes, reading speed will be influenced by their ability to grasp a word or idea and pass on to the next. Interpretation is related to purpose. Students must have a purpose in all their reading activities. These exercises establish that purpose for them. For all reading, students should decide upon that purpose, mentally ask themselves questions, then read to answer those questions.

The *perception* exercises are designed to develop the ability to "see" words correctly, to discriminate between similar words, and to identify them with split-second accuracy. If a word cannot be seen correctly, its meaning will be distorted or misinterpreted.

The *comprehension* exercises are designed to improve students' ability to extract meaning accurately with rapid understanding. To read rapidly, it is necessary to comprehend or understand the specific meaning of a word, a phrase, or a sentence in the shortest possible time.

Remind students that they should not worship speed for speed's sake! Reading speed doesn't function in isolation. Speed is determined by comprehension; the reader grasps one idea and hurries on to the next. Similarly, comprehension is determined by vocabulary and other factors. Practice that stresses comprehension yields greater gains for both speed and comprehension than practice that stresses speed alone. In this respect, this course differs from most others that would promote the false goal of speed for speed's sake.

What Does Research Say About Speed Reading?

Nearly every month, local newspapers and magazines publish reports and advertisements from commercial companies offering "rapid reading" courses "guaranteed" to improve one's reading rate and comprehension. Some companies have stated that the student could attain reading rates of 20,000 to 30,000 words per minute. Others have been more temperate in suggesting the possibility of attaining a mere rate of 2,000 to 3,000 words per minute. Of course, there is a charge involved, something like $350 to $500 for a six-week, one-night-per-week course of study!

Other newspapers have reported individuals mastering reading rates of 20,000 to 40,000 words per minute! One issue of a midwestern newspaper even reported the success of a girl who "read" 50,000 words per minute with nearly "100 percent comprehension"! If these claims were true, just imagine, it would be possible to read *Gone with the Wind* in approximately 10 minutes! It goes without saying that this is an impossible task.

The question immediately arises as to how much of this propaganda is fact and how much is fiction. Recently, reading researchers decided to answer this question using well-designed scientific methods. To do so, they first agreed upon a definition as to what reading is. In ordinary usage, reading means acquiring the intended meaning from printed or written language symbols. It is this definition the research scientists used in examining the above claims.

Completing their research, the scientists agreed that it is physiologically impossible to read more than 800 to 900 words per minute. Note that the definition does not imply the process of skimming or scanning, both of which are entirely different modes of securing information. As for the evidence, it was discovered and authenticated that (1) the shortest effective fixation in reading is 166 milliseconds as determined by photographic evidence of eye movements; (2) the time required for the saccade (movement of the eye to the next fixation) is 33 milliseconds; and (3) the maximum number of words that the eye can possibly see with a single fixation during continuous reading (probably 2.5 to 3.0 words) equals only three words every fifth second. Because there are 300 such intervals in one minute, only 3×300 or 900 words per minute can be actually read. Obviously, this must be the upper limit due to the difficulty of maintaining the rate of five fixations per second for an extended period.

Thus, assuming that a reader can recognize and comprehend a maximum visual span of three words per fixation, and there are no regressive eye movements (rereading), an individual can read at the rate of approximately 15 words per second or 900 words per minute. Any speed greater than this involves omitting lines—a technique recognized by most authorities as skimming. Reading is not a process in which relatively large portions of the reading material are skipped.

What is skimming? Skimming is the vertical skill in which the eyes of the reader move rapidly down the page in a manner to locate a word in the dictionary or a number in the phone book. Scanning is a process in which the eyes quickly survey written material to identify the main idea. In practice, it may be necessary only to read the first line or sentence of a paragraph and skim the rest of the material looking for key words, and thus infer the less important details surrounding significant words. But more about these two processes in succeeding lessons.

So, if we accept the commonly recognized definition of reading as our criterion and apply it to research findings, we can be assured that the maximum number of words read can be no more than 800 to 900 words per minute—newspaper feature stories, Sunday supplements, and advertisements notwithstanding!

You'll be interested to know that the reading material used in the advertised commercial speed reading courses consists of light, easy content written at an elementary school level— usually fifth and sixth grade. Never will you find copies of a technical journal, *The Decline of the West,* or history or physics texts.

Now that we're squared away on what can and cannot be accomplished in a speed reading course, let's take a look at what improved reading speed will do for the average student once speed skills have been mastered. The following example is taken from a typical assignment of 10,000 words in an American history course.

Reading Rate	Reading Time
50 words per minute	3 hours, 20 minutes
100 words per minute	1 hour, 40 minutes
200 words per minute	50 minutes
250 words per minute	40 minutes
300 words per minute	34 minutes
400 words per minute	25 minutes

Note that, as reading rate increases, the total time decreases in geometric proportion. The time difference between a student reading an entire chapter at 200 words per minute and the one reading at 300 words per minute is only 16 minutes. However, the time difference between the student reading the chapter at 100 words per minute and the one struggling along at 50 words per minute is one hour and 40 minutes. Increasing one's speed from 50 to 100 words per minute provides a reduction of 50 percent in the amount of time required to cover a reading assignment.

It should be remembered that in any secondary school class there exists a considerable spread of reading rates. The average would probably range from 100 to 300 words per minute. Although a high reading rate might be satisfying to one's personal and recreational reading, a maximum effective rate is most important when working on assigned reading tasks. This course will help students achieve that goal.

What You Should Know About Reading—Student Inventory

As a student, you should know something about the concepts and skills developed in this book. By doing so, you are more likely to begin your speed reading course free from false notions and unfounded attitudes. Not only will your motivation improve, but you will be better able to understand your strengths and weaknesses as a rapid reader. Consequently, we have included a personal inventory of your reading ability—an inventory that will help you understand the objectives of this course.

A.   Definition

Speed reading is training to improve your reading rate and efficiency without loss of comprehension.

B.   The Physical Factors of Reading

1.   *Vocalization and Subvocalization:* A condition of sounding words with the lips or in the larynx. Both vocalization and subvocalization are a form of reading word by word, thus creating an excessively slow reading rate.

When reading silently, do you form words without sounding them? _____

2.   *Eye Span:* The amount of type or number of printed symbols seen in one eye stop. A narrow eye span limits both rate and comprehension.

Do you read word by word? _____

3.   *Vision:* In reading, an individual's eyes stop briefly and then move on to another stop. Without these stops, there would be no recognition of printed symbols.

Have your eyes been examined recently? _____

4.   *Regressions:* The practice of rereading or involuntarily going over material already read. Regressing is a handicap to reading efficiency.

Do you reread to identify something missed? _____

C. **Psychological Factors**

1. *Your Attitude:* Most students want to read faster although many unconsciously resist change in their reading habits. Why this resistance?

    a. Because they have the notion that "slow readers get the most out of their reading." Research disproves this idea.

    b. Because elementary schoolteachers enforced the rule that "every word must be read."

    c. Because of lack of confidence in earlier reading tasks. Lack of confidence leads to discouragement.

        Did you experience any of the above in your earlier school experience? _____

2. *Your Motivation:* Reading is the basis of most learning in the secondary school. A perpetually slow and inefficient reader is forever handicapped. Improvement in reading speed contributes to better grades, personal satisfaction, and improved confidence.

    Do you really believe these advantages are valuable to your reading efficiency? _____

D. **Vocabulary**

Vocabulary consists of the words we understand or use in all verbal and written communication. A limited vocabulary is an important cause of delayed or inaccurate comprehension. Why is vocabulary so important? Because a facility with words is an excellent predictor of college or career success and serves as the basic foundation for comprehension. Vocabulary *can* be improved.

Is your general and technical vocabulary excellent, good, or below par? _____

E. **Concentration**

Concentration is the ability to direct one's attention to a specific purpose in the reading process. To concentrate, one must mentally develop a purpose for reading.

Do you easily become absorbed in your reading task without wasting time and without being easily distracted? _____

Are you able to concentrate for lengthy periods of time without your mind wandering? _____

F. Retention

Retention is the amount of time that it takes to comprehend and retain material over a period of time.

Do you remember content that is really important and must be available for recall? _____

G. Word Analysis

Word analysis is the ability to decode or "attack" new and unfamiliar words.

Are you able to divide words into their proper syllables? _____

Are you able to recognize root words? _____

Do you know the most common prefixes and suffixes? _____

H. Comprehension

Comprehension means the complete understanding of what is read.

Do you think about what you hope to learn before you start reading? _____

Are you able to identify quickly main ideas in a paragraph? _____

Are you able to read accurately graphs, charts, and tables? _____

Do you know how to use context clues to determine meaning of unfamiliar words? _____

Is it easy to explain to others material you have just read? _____

I. Flexible Reading Rate

Reading rate is the rate at which you can read easy, moderate, and difficult material. Flexibility is the adaptation of reading rate to purpose. This is one of the most profitable characteristics of efficient reading. Flexibility indicates that the reader has *several reading rates*, not one single reading rate.

Do you adjust your reading rate to the difficulty of the material? _____

And now, please estimate (guess) what your reading rate is at this moment in words per minute (wpm). _____

To the Teacher

Read Carefully

The amount of time a teacher devotes to the course will vary with the individual instructor. In practice, the writer finds that a short class period devoted to a full explanation of the discussion unit plus the completion of the exercises and their scoring constitutes a time period of approximately 20 to 25 minutes. This time may be extended if additional reading exercises and practice are desired. Providing the bulk of the practice material must ultimately rest with the student, for it is the individual who is improving his or her reading speed. Newspapers, light fiction, magazines, and novels are all good sources for practice material. Such additions lead to greater achievement and are highly recommended.

THE ADMINISTRATION OF THE PROGRAM

Beginning: The class period begins with a distribution of the reproducible pages to each student, followed by a full discussion of the day's topic taken from the daily discussion unit. Because of the nature of the exercises, students should be cautioned *not* to examine the exercises found on the following pages. At the completion of the course, reproducible pages should be given to the students for future review and practice.

Exercises: The exercises include skill practice material in interpretation, perception, and comprehension. These are followed by the story selections.

Timing: Since all exercises are done under forced time conditions, greater accuracy is achieved by the administrator's use of a stopwatch or the second hand of a watch. If the second hand method is used, begin all exercises on the 60-second mark. This procedure makes for simplified timing.

Using a stopwatch: The teacher begins *all* exercises with the command "Ready—begin," at which time the stopwatch is activated. When a student has completed his exercise, he should raise his hand. Glancing at the watch, the teacher gives him the time in seconds. Because of the intense levels of concentration, this verbal notation in no way interferes with nor interrupts the student's efficiency. Once the student has been notified of the time, he enters it in the proper blank at the bottom of the exercise, waiting until all students have completed their work. Succeeding exercises (Perception and Interpretation) are done in the same manner.

Using a wall chart: Should a stopwatch not be available, it is possible to provide timed information to students by using a wall chart. On the chalkboard, make a copy of the following chart, which, with a watch or wall clock containing a second hand, provides an adequate timing device.

The teacher begins *all* exercises with the command: "Ready—begin." By watching the clock or stopwatch, you can move your hand down the wall chart in an appropriate manner, indicating the correct time slot. Upon completing the exercise, each student looks at the time shown by the teacher's hand or pointer and enters the time in the proper blank at the bottom of the exercise, then waits until all students have completed their work. The two succeeding exercises (Perception and Comprehension) are done in the same manner. Once students have completed their three exercises (Interpretation, Perception, and Comprehension), have them exchange their books at which time the teacher reads the answers. Books are then returned to their owners. It would be profitable to discuss wrong answers in the Interpretation and Comprehension exercises. Students should be encouraged to use the dictionary to confirm their choices.

Scoring for the Interpretation, Perception, and Comprehension exercises is done in this manner: Multiply the number of errors by 5, then subtract the product (answer) from 100. This provides you with the correct score for the exercise. Appropriate entries of both time in seconds and scores are entered in Figures 1, 2, and 3 in the Appendix.

Although time limits are posted at the top of each of the three exercises, these figures are meant to serve only as guides, not as cutoff points for the class. Even though some students may not complete their exercises within the stated time, *permit them to finish*, but impress upon them the need for attempting to reach these goals in each succeeding lesson. The time limits *do include* reading the directions.

Story selections: Once three selections are completed, the *first* of the two story selections is begun in the same manner, except that exactly 3 minutes are provided for reading each story; this time limit also includes answering the questions. Should a student complete the selection before the 3-minute limit, he or she should wait until all students have completed their story (within the time limit of 3 minutes, of course).

On the *second* story, the procedure is modified somewhat. This selection is started in the same manner, but *after 30 seconds,* class reading is stopped. Each student counts the number of words he or she has read in the 30-second period, then doubles that figure, giving the student a gross words per minute (GWPM) score. This is entered at the bottom of the story page in the proper blank. Once everyone has computed his or her GWPM score, again start the class together so as to complete the reading. The remaining time amounts to 2½ minutes (a total of 3 minutes for the entire selection). After the 3-minute period, students exchange their books for scoring. The teacher reads the answers, books are returned to their owners, and the teacher discusses the answers with the class.

For the story selections, each item has a value of 10. The number multiplied by 10 gives the total score. Scores of *both* stories are then averaged, the average score being placed in the Average Comprehension (Avg. Comp.) blank at the bottom of the second story. Then the GWPM score is multiplied by the Average Comprehension Score (Avg. Comp.). By dropping off the last two digits (dividing by 100), an effective words per minute (EWPM) score is obtained. These three scores—GWPM, Avg. Comp., and EWPM—are all transferred to Table 1 in the Appendix. The EWPM and Avg. Comp. scores are then entered in Figure 4. This figure provides a graphic representation of progress. The formula used here is also found at the bottom of each second story selection as well as in Table 1. Example: If the GWPM is 220 and the Average Comprehension Score is 80, the effective words per minute score would be 220 × 80 or 176 (176.00) EWPM.

Upon completion of the course, the pretest (Lesson One) EWPM score is subtracted from the posttest (Lesson Fifteen) EWPM score. Multiply the difference by 100 (simply add two zeros to the difference), then divide by the pretest score. This quotient is the percent of improvement made for the course shown in EWPM. An example follows.

Posttest score	450 EWPM
Pretest score	−200 EWPM
Difference	250 EWPM
Multiplied by 100	25000
Divided by pretest score	200 EWPM
Improvement	125%

Looking back: Students may look back at the story for their answers. The amount of referral or looking back will depend upon the amount of reinforcement needed to remember certain details and the strength of the student's understanding of the selection's major ideas. In the final analysis, it is what the student does with the stated facts that really counts. In looking back, the student is actually building memory skills more efficiently because he or she is forced to remember what to look for. Furthermore, this practice provides an excellent opportunity for building skimming skills.

FINDING THE GRADE LEVEL

The following method is often used for determining the degree of difficulty (grade level) for reading materials:

1. Choose five and one-half pages that are as representative as possible.

2. In each sentence, count one for each word of one or two syllables. Count three for each word of three or more syllables. Count numbers and proper names as one. Count each clause of a compound sentence as a separate sentence.

3. Divide the count for each sentence by two. The result is the grade level for the sentence.

4. Add the grade levels for all sentences and divide by the number of sentences. The answer is the grade level for the half page.

5. Average the grade levels for the five and one half pages. The answer is roughly the grade level for the book.

6. Write the grade level on the slip of paper and put it inside the cover.

Lesson One

What Is an Efficient Reader?

Background

What is an efficient reader? Reading efficiency is based upon many factors. A common weakness found in many secondary students is the tendency to read all materials at the same rate. In many situations, this is wasted effort. A knowledgeable and efficient reader will have developed the ability to read different materials at appropriate and vastly different rates. In other words, the efficient reader changes her pace—some passages are read rapidly and others more slowly according to the reader's purpose and background in the selection's content. This ability to adjust one's reading rate to the material is basic to the improvement of reading rate and is called "flexibility." This means that to improve rate, emphasis must be placed upon flexibility in applying any reading skill and adjusting rates to varied purposes and needs.

Just as car drivers vary their speed according to their purpose, weather, and road conditions, so do efficient readers. Driving a patient to the hospital is obviously quite different from taking a Sunday afternoon drive. The purposes for each activity are different. Both, however, must be done efficiently. In doing so, much effort is saved. Once one's reading rate has been determined, speed and comprehension improve, saving hours of time and effort. The foregoing discussion indicates that if students are to develop an efficient rate, they must understand that all materials are not meant to be read at the same speed nor are they to be treated alike. Many reading assignments must be studied carefully and with a high degree of thoroughness. Others, obviously, are to be read with rapidity and a light touch.

Reading Rate

What then is an efficient reading rate? Most certainly, it is not reading everything at the same speed. It is not reading every word at a slow speed. In fact, reading some materials in a word-by-word manner may actually interfere with comprehension. We have abandoned the idea that all words should be read with equal emphasis. Comprehension does not improve using this method, nor does it improve memory.

Furthermore, unlike the early reading instruction we each received, everything printed is not worth reading or remembering. Newspaper content is an excellent example of what we're talking about.

On the other hand, everything printed should not be read at fantastic speeds. Let's assume a student tries reading a science assignment at 500 words per minute (wpm), never pausing to define unfamiliar words. Could the content be mastered? Of course not, so why waste time? Science, like several other subjects, requires knowledge of specific technical words. Moreover, extensive details cry for attention. It takes time and effort to identify and absorb technical details.

So if an expert's reading rate is neither fast nor slow, what is an efficient rate? Here's the first basic principle for developing increased reading speed: *An efficient reading rate is one that suits the reader's purpose!* It may be slow, say 100 to 200 words per minute; it may be 200 to 400 wpm; or it may be 500 to 600 wpm. Once purpose has been determined and implemented, almost any reading speed may be classified as efficient. Remind students to first identify their purpose, recognize the selection's level of difficulty, determine the extent of their familiarity with the subject matter—then read!

Purpose

When studying most textbook assignments, the reader's purpose is to master certain facts and concepts. Many assignments may be read at a slow pace. Because one reads for details in science, reading rate may be no more than 200 wpm. In social studies, however, where the primary purpose is to gather general ideas, speed, no doubt, may increase to 400 wpm. Because each word, symbol, and concept in math is important, this material should be read much more slowly. In literature, reading rates increase because one is generally interested in main ideas, impressions, and literary flavor. Due to its emotional nature, some drama and most poetry must be read slowly to savor and absorb the full meaning of every word.

Reading rates for recreational reading materials vary with purpose also. If the reader is interested in keeping current with general information, rate should be high. If, however, one reads for specific details, speed diminishes. Conversely, if the purpose is to identify and enlarge upon an opposing point of view, rate may speed up again, or slow down, depending upon the selection's level of difficulty. In every case, reading rate should be determined by the reader's purpose. With these thoughts in mind, students might ask themselves these or similar questions: What does the teacher want me to know about this assignment? What is the writer trying to say? What do these words add up to? These and similar questions help establish purpose. Once this principle has been established in your mind, you're well on your way to improving your reading speed with confidence.

Reading is a type of work, albeit a pleasurable form of work for some of us. As work, this means that efficient reading requires an output of energy proportionate to the task. But if all the reading materials were of equal difficulty, then all reading situations should be approached in precisely the same manner. However, this is not the case.

Lesson Two

Common Reading Faults

Background

We have implied that efficient readers race through an ordinary novel or newspaper with ease. Their eyes move quickly over the lines of print with a high degree of comprehension. Efficient readers fully grasp what they read and retain it for long periods of time. They realize the importance of establishing purpose and that different materials are read at varying rates. Expert readers always predetermine their purpose, then read for that purpose whether it be for pleasure, study, information, or a combination of all three. Efficient readers also make mental notes of what is read, particularly on technical or difficult material; and they concentrate intensively on the text. If the doubt persists that students won't remember or understand as well as if they read more slowly, they should discard that doubt. Students will comprehend just as much, and, in many cases, understand more than what they do now. Students must, however, rid themselves of several common reading faults. Let's take a look at some of the more prominent ones.

Vocalization

Slow readers tend to have a variety of bad habits that can be corrected. Though some are physical in nature, others have been learned. Whatever the cause, it is possible to overcome each of them with reasonable ease. One of the most common problems is demonstrated by the individual who thinks it's necessary to pronounce each word on the printed page. This is called "vocalization" and is done in a very subtle and soft manner. Contrast the average thinking rate of up to 60,000 words per minute with the average oral speaking rate of 150 words per minute, then compare these with the average silent reading rate of 250 words per minute. It becomes apparent that pronouncing words to oneself automatically slows reading rate to about one-half the average silent speed. Vocalization is easily eliminated through conscious effort. If this proves too much of a mental chore for some students, ask them to put a pencil in their mouths as they read. This technique inhibits the physical action of the lips. Failing this, they could try chewing gum. Both techniques make it impossible to vocalize when reading silently.

Subvocalization

Closely related to vocalization is the more difficult problem of "subvocalization." This is a form of silent reading in which there is no visible physical movement, although words are actually formed in the larynx. Although the lips, tongue, and vocal cords do not move, inner speech persists. While this is a difficult problem to overcome, it is not an impossibility. Students should recognize the difficulty for what it is, then read rapidly under timed conditions at a rate too rapid to permit subvocalization. The students' aim is to visually observe words instantly to obtain their impact directly. If this fails, and students continue to subvocalize, they should try directing questions to the text or carry on a mental dialogue with the writer. Above all, students should not passively mouth the writer's words.

Pointing

Another common problem is shown by the student who persists in pointing at words with a finger, pencil, or ruler. This type of behavior only slows down the reader's rate and subconsciously focuses attention on an artificial device that does nothing but slow reading speed. The prime purpose in reading is to concentrate on what the writer is attempting to communicate, not on the location of words on a page. Encourage these students to try folding their hands and making their eyes do the work.

Head Movement

Head movement is another common fault that slows rate. Aiming the nose at the printed word does not increase rate or comprehension. Ask each head mover to hold his or her chin firmly in hand while reading. Alternatively, these students could place one hand by the side of their heads. This will call attention to the fact that their heads do indeed move as their eyes pursue the printed text. Remind students to force their eyes to widen their visual span. Breaking bad habits may be annoying at first, but with practice, can be overcome successfully.

Other important aspects of poor reading that are not of a physical nature include the inability to read at high levels of comprehension, deficient vocabulary, inability to identify and grasp main ideas, and difficulty in identifying significant details. Each of these topics will be dealt with in succeeding lessons.

Fixation

When our eyes move along a line of print, they do not glide smoothly as we might imagine. Instead, they make a series of short, jerky movements at every word or two for a brief pause. Each of these pauses, or stops, is called a "fixation." The more fixations per line, the slower the reading rate. If it were not for these stops, we would see nothing because the movement of our eyes between each fixation is so rapid that anything "seen" during the movement is nothing more than a rapid blur. Fortunately, the brain contains a little mechanism that blots out the blur. Otherwise, we would wind up with severe headaches. Consequently, we see words only when our eyes are stopped during the fixation periods. When our eyes do stop, the area seen is called the eye span or recognition span. Eye movement cameras indicate that the average recognition span of most readers is slightly more than one word. Slow and inefficient readers make word-by-word fixations that look something like this:

When our eyes move along a line of print, they

do not glide smoothly as we might imagine.

The recognition span of some readers is so narrow that their eyes actually "fix" on individual letters or syllables in each word. These readers pause for every word in a line of print. Of course, the reader can't read rapidly because he or she is pinned down with each letter, syllable, or word. On the other hand, fast readers have learned to take in an average of two or more words with each fixation, thus doubling their reading speed. The fast reader's rate looks something like this:

Fast readers see several words with each fixation.

It is advantageous for the reader to *decrease* the number of fixations per line and *increase*, or widen, the recognition span. By doing so, reading time can be cut in half. Although some reading programs would have you believe that it is possible to see 4 or 5 words in some fixations (some even go so far as to suggest that it is possible to see an entire paragraph, page, or even "globs" of print), eye movement camera records indicate that most efficient readers see approximately 2.5 to 3 words per fixation.

Discovery

The credit for the discovery that human eyes do not move in smooth, even intervals but in a series of jerky movements with pauses between has been given to a scientist by the name of Javal, who in 1878 made a significant discovery by simply watching a schoolchild read a book. Javal's predecessors had assumed the common belief of "sweeping the eyes along a line of print." Javal found not a steady sweep, but a series of little jumps (saccadic movements) with intervening fixation pauses. Another scientist by the name of Delabarre affixed a plaster of paris cup to the eyes of some students. Embedded in the plaster cup was a thin wire that Delabarre wet with ink. As the students read, a written record of how their eyes performed was left upon the printed matter. Javal had achieved the same results by observing the eyes of a person who was reading.

Suggestion

Today, it doesn't take a scientist to prove this point. You can easily observe someone's eye movements and actually try to count the number of fixations made per line. Using a piece of 9" × 12" cardboard, attach two paragraphs of 6 to 10 lines of reading material of appropriate difficulty, one paragraph just above the center of the cardboard and the other just below the center. In the middle of the cardboard, cut a small hole ¼" to ⅜" in diameter. Hold the cardboard at the proper reading distance directly in front of the student and place your eyes immediately behind the opening. You now have an advantageous point from which to see the successive movements and fixation pauses of the student's eyes as he or she reads the material on the cardboard. Fix your attention on the dividing line between the iris and the white of the student's eye. This method reduces the distraction that would occur if you were to make a direct observation of the subject.

By using this procedure, you will be able to see quickly the subject's eye movements and get some idea of the number of fixations per line. You may even see an occasional "regression." A regression is a backward movement of the eye, indicating the subject is rereading a word or phrase. Generally speaking, regressions are a sign of inefficient reading, although most of us do make a few upon occasion. But remember, fast readers make few regressions, slow readers make many. Remind students to force themselves to read all practice materials just once. They should try not to reread. By doing so, they will begin to overcome another faulty reading habit.

Build Your Vocabulary

Comprehension

What's the status of the students' vocabularies? Is it adequate for daily reading tasks? Are students ever puzzled by an unfamiliar word in their reading assignments? If students have problems with the decoding of strange words and their comprehension isn't what it should be, then this section is for them.

To read rapidly and efficiently, students must instantly recognize and define thousands of words, some never seen before, others whose meaning or context simply escapes them. Good students always have a better vocabulary than poor students. Because vocabulary is a comprehension tool, the knowledgeable student is better able to discriminate among the fine meanings of words. The expert reads faster and more efficiently because perception of word meaning is accomplished with split-second accuracy. By doing so, comprehension improves. Students have already discovered in previous examples that failure to understand a word slows down reading rate. It does because word meaning is intrinsic to overall comprehension. If students want to become more competent readers and increase their overall speed, then they must become masters of words. They can do this by expanding their vocabularies.

Context Clues

Building one's vocabulary doesn't mean studying long lists of rare and technical words. The best way to develop vocabulary is to read, and read extensively. Students must pay attention to new words; skipping them never does the job. Often, the meaning of a phrase or sentence depends upon that unfamiliar word. In fact, the sentence concerned may contain the main idea or an important detail, one we can't afford to miss. The first thing to do when meeting an unfamiliar word is determine whether the word's meaning is explained by the context of the sentence. It may be explained, for example, by a modifier, restatement, or even an example. In some cases, the word may possibly be defined in a following sentence. Students must be alert to context clues—clues to sentence meaning.

Dictionaries

Remind students to develop the dictionary habit. If the context doesn't provide a clue to the word's meaning, students should look it up. Several dictionaries are punched and may be placed in a looseleaf notebook. Others are small enough to be carried in a pocket. Another practical idea is for students to keep a vocabulary notebook and divide it into two sections. In one section, they should jot down words of general nature—words commonly found in history, literature, civics, newspapers, and magazines. In the other section, students should jot down technical words—words that have special meaning in a specialized subject area such as physics, biology, chemistry, and geography. General vocabulary words can be found in most good dictionaries. Technical words are found in specialized or unabridged dictionaries. Before they know it, students will have a personal dictionary containing many active words—words they customarily meet in everyday reading assignments, words that have specialized use, and words that students formerly recognized in a vague manner but whose meaning they were never quite sure of.

Another fascinating method of vocabulary improvement is to develop an interest in word origins. Knowing something about the origin of a word makes it more easily remembered. For example, the word "pencil" comes from Latin and originally meant "from a little tail," and "salary" meant "salt money." "Taxicab" literally meant "a carriage that bounced like a goat," and "senate" meant a "meeting of old men." Encourage students to check their bookstore; many books are available that provide the origin of commonly used English words.

Word Parts

Here's another good idea: Help students become conscious of root words, prefixes, and suffixes. Remind them that it's possible to double their vocabularies by learning no more than a couple of dozen prefixes. It takes no more than 14 of the most common prefixes to account for over 80 percent of the prefixes used in a 20,000-word vocabulary! Furthermore, one fourth of the words in a 20,000-word dictionary have prefixes. Of course, the English language has borrowed words from many sources and languages and will continue to do so. For example, "divan" comes from the Arabic; "moose" from the American Indian; "magic" from the Greek; and "sari" from Hindi. Our prefixes and suffixes also came from foreign languages. Students should learn the most common. If they do, students can double their vocabularies overnight.

List the 14 most common prefixes and their meanings: ab- (from), ad- (to), be- (by), com- (with), de- (from), dis- (apart), en- (in), ex- (out), in- (into), pre- (before), pro- (in front of), re- (back or again), sub- (under), and un- (not).

Lesson Five

Reading Purpose Is the Key to Comprehension

Plan of Action

Many students sit down after the evening meal, assemble their textbooks, and proceed to "read" their assignments. Many do this simply because the teacher assigned the material. Time spent on "reading" assignments in this manner can be wasted effort. Looking at words isn't reading. The process requires much more skill than that. To be a successful and efficient reader, students must use several specialized reading skills to achieve success. First of all, they must concentrate on the selective content. More than that, their purpose in reading must be established *before* tackling any printed materials. The interpretation exercises in this book have been designed to help students establish this most important key to successful reading practice. The exercises by themselves will not do the job; the most important ingredient is the student and how he or she approaches reading activities. We suggest that students learn immediately how to develop an aggressive, searching attitude toward all printed materials. They need to decide beforehand *why* they are reading. The answer becomes their purpose. Reading purpose depends upon the information students want to gain and the amount of time they have to secure it. Once established, they should read in terms of that goal. Remind students to avoid distractions. They should approach reading with a question, read, and come up with an answer. Students should create a plan of action with reading: establish their purpose, ask themselves mental questions, then read for the answers. Their purpose will be satisfied, the answers their own reward.

Purpose

Purpose has a great deal to do with reading success, as it has with most everything we attempt. There are as many good reasons for reading as there are things to read—even classroom assignments! Purpose determines what students will read, the reason "why," and the manner in which they pursue this activity.

Remind students to listen to the questions and directions of a reading assignment, then, as they read, to search specifically for the things asked for. When no directions or questions are given, students should ask themselves their own questions before they begin. They should look for the answers as they read. Students are, in part, setting their own purpose when they ask themselves questions about an assignment. It is these questions that serve as guides for what they're attempting to achieve.

An easy way to establish purpose is to convert the title, chapter heading, or subheading into a question, then read to answer those questions. Often the opening paragraph explains the theme of a chapter and provides clues for developing purpose-setting questions. The closing paragraph often provides a purposeful base for formulating questions because that one paragraph generally summarizes all points covered in the selection. Students should use all of the author's aids—titles, subtitles, pictures, captions, opening and closing paragraphs—to help establish purposeful questions.

Reading Speeds

Once purpose has been established, the students' reading speed will be regulated by that purpose and the difficulty of the material. Obviously, the more they know about the subject before they read it, the more they'll get out of it and the faster they'll read. Having established their purpose, students must now match that goal with one of three reading speeds: (1) study rate, (2) skimming rate, and (3) recreational rate. The study rate is the slowest of all reading speeds and is used for difficult material. It is also the one that provides the highest degree of understanding due to its concern with main ideas and details. Too often, students tend to use the study rate for all reading tasks, when, in reality, they should be using a study technique such as the P-Q-R-S-T, S-Q-3-R, or any other tested, organized approach to studying. I like the P-Q-R-S-T study method and will discuss it in full detail in a later lesson.

Recreational or leisure-time reading rates are those used when reading for pleasure. This is where increased rapid reading speeds really come into their own. Typical reading materials may consist of detective stories, light novels, or adventure stories. Vocabulary and writing patterns of this type of material are usually adequate enough to tell the story, but are not too complex. The main purpose in reading such materials is to be entertained and not instructed.

Skimming is reading at the fastest possible speed to get important information quickly. Skimming is a selective process of "looking and reading"; one looks for necessary specifics (this is purpose), then pauses to read. When skimming, the eyes sweep down the printed page without actually reading every word, searching for important facts or significant phrases that coincide with one's purpose.

There you have it. Students must learn to read different kinds of materials in different ways. They must ask themselves these kinds of questions: What type of reading material is this? What is my purpose in reading this material? What reading rate best suits my purpose and difficulty of the selection? But remember, students must define their purpose *before* they begin, then utilize an appropriate rate. If they follow this simple plan, they will be surprised by the results.

Previewing

Background

The purpose of a movie or television preview is to arouse the viewers' interest, stimulate their curiosity, and provide them with some idea as to what the next program will be. Before you take a vacation, consult road maps, travel brochures, and assemble clothing and travel gear. Before an expert golfer plays a new course, he or she walks the fairway, inspects the lie of the greens, and spots the hazards. In each case, a preview is being made of the activity to establish a perspective. The same sort of perspective should be established by rapid readers before they begin each nonfiction reading assignment.

Built-in Clues

Let's assume students are assigned Chapter 14 for tomorrow's history lesson. They should begin the previewing process by first reading the introduction (if there is one), or the first paragraph. Then they should quickly skim through the material, turning the pages as they glance at the headings, subheadings, illustrations, and other graphic material. Students should take note of the chapter's length (number of pages) and the subject matter covered. Does the chapter cover a specific period of time? If so, what period? Then they should read the summary; this reviews the most important points in the chapter without involving the reader in details. Perhaps it would be a good idea to point out the importance of headings. Most students pay little attention to these bold-face or italicized clues to comprehension. Headings and subheadings constitute major topics of the author's outline. They reveal every important topic in the chapter's structure. Often a preview of subtitles will tell the reader all he or she needs to know about the selection. At other times, subtitles serve as stimulus clues to develop interest, thus providing a basis for readers' purpose questions. It is important for students to pay close attention to these built-in clues. Authors spend long hours organizing their books and chapters in this manner to provide readers with organized expectations and to make their task easier. Students shouldn't ignore these useful guideposts to previewing.

Having completed a preview of the chapter's content, students should have a sufficient understanding of what the assignment is all about. This is the outline to be mentally filled in as students pursue the reading task.

When previewing a book, students should begin by reading the preface. In it, the writer quickly provides an idea as to why the book was written and what he or she attempts to do in it. The preface also provides clues as to whether the book is right for the reader; it may even explain what background or preparation is required to fully comprehend its content. Students should examine the table of contents carefully because it contains an outline of all material covered within the book's covers. It also provides a framework for important ideas and supporting details. Later, when students read the book, they should refer occasionally to the table of contents. In doing so, their knowledge of the book's organization and development will be reinforced. Next, students should quickly leaf through the book's pages, examining chapter headings and skimming first paragraphs and chapter summaries. Regardless of how long the preview takes, it is worth every minute of it. Remind students that they should not neglect this important secret employed by fast, efficient readers.

The preview doesn't take much time, perhaps three or four minutes for a chapter, and perhaps no more than an hour for previewing a complete text. Its primary purpose is to obtain a general idea of what the chapter or book is all about. With practice and experience, previewing proves to be an important key to comprehending difficult material and retaining it more permanently. It really works!

Non-textual Materials

But previewing isn't reserved for surveying nonfiction books. It is a useful tool to use when reading magazine articles, fiction, and other non-textual materials. Here are some useful techniques for students to use when reading these materials. First, read the title and any subtitles accompanying it. These provide a general idea of the subject. Often the author's name will spark the reader's interest and perhaps offer a clue as to the content's authenticity. If there are charts, photographs, or illustrations, the reader should look at them carefully. They provide a mental picture of the selection. If there is boldface type and numbered points, students should give these attention also. Remind students to read all captions; they are very important. Now students can read the first few paragraphs; these contain the writer's approach to the subject. Students should immediately move on to the final paragraphs where conclusions are reached. Once students have completed the preview, they will have the gist of the article. Then they will know whether the selection is worth reading. In addition, they will have paved the way for better retention of the material. Best of all, they've done it in the shortest possible time.

As for newspapers, there is no necessity to preview material. The reporter has already done it with headlines and subheads. The most important facts of the story are found in the first few sentences or paragraphs. In succeeding paragraphs, supplementary facts become less and less important.

Read in Thought Units

Visual Span

Another basic skill useful in developing reading speed is the ability to read in thought units. This means being able to take visual "bites" as the eyes move along each line of print. We have explained that one's eyes read in a series of stops or fixations, jerking along to the right after each stop to take in the next portion of the line. Since we read only when the eyes have stopped, the more words taken in at each fixation, the fewer stops will be required, and the faster we read. By increasing the eye's visual span of recognition, the faster the eyes cover a line of print.

Test students' present visual span by having them focus their eyes on every fifth word in the next line of print. Even though their eyes will be fixed on a single *word*, their visual span should *permit* the reading of a word or words on the left and right of that target word. As students practice expanding or widening their peripheral vision, more words will be absorbed with each fixation.

Thought Reading

Of course, if students are reading a list of spelling words, it is necessary to read word by word. But in normal reading, words are held together in phrases, clauses, and sentences. Each is a thought unit. The idea is to take in visually as much as is physiologically possible of each unit. Not only does thought reading increase reading speed, it also improves comprehension. Word-by-word readers achieve their information at too slow a pace. Word-by-word readers can think much faster than they read, and because they can, their mind wanders and they lose comprehension.

We have already seen that rapid readers are not word callers and are not able to read a complete sentence with one fixation. How, then, is it possible to use the construction of a sentence to improve reading speed? Although sentences are built with individual words, words are grouped in thought units. These units are natural blocks of understanding through which the meaning of a sentence is developed.

Blocks of Communication

What does a thought unit look like? Fortunately, our punctuation system provides markers for many comprehension thought units; we might call them blocks of communication. They may take the form of a prepositional phrase, a noun and its modifying adjective, a subordinate clause, a relative pronoun and its verb, or it may be an article and its succeeding noun or adjective. Between units, one can generally find a break or mental pause. These pauses occur so the reader may capitalize on reading in thought units. By connecting thought units, comprehension becomes clearer and more understandable.

Suggestion

Meaning is seldom contained in the form of a single word. Slow readers and word callers have great difficulty in deriving meaning from reading assignments because they see words as single entities. Fast readers see words in groups or clusters. It's no wonder that a word caller's comprehension level is low; all sense of the sentence is lost by the time it has been read. It might be interesting to see an example of text divided into thought units. Show students a portion of Lincoln's Gettysburg Address as it might look in thought unit form:

Fourscore / and seven years ago / our fathers / brought forth /

on this continent / a new nation / conceived in liberty /

and dedicated / to the proposition / that all men / are created /

equal. / Now / we are engaged / in a great / civil war /

testing whether / that nation / or any nation / so conceived /

After students have read it, ask them if they noticed a certain rhythm as their eyes moved from line to line. If so, then they might agree that this form of reading could be called "rhythmic reading." But we don't have to settle for historic texts because most prose, hymns, and poetry provide excellent examples of texts that have already been divided into thought units. Students may have a little difficulty at first in dividing sentences into thought units, but with practice, they will find a comfortable rhythmic pattern.

Remind students that all thought units are not of the same length. Some may be no more than one word, some two, and others may contain three or four words. The idea is to read more than one word at a time, conditioned by the text's natural groupings. Students should start dividing sentences into their natural units, but begin with easy materials, making sure the units are small. They should gradually tackle more complex sentences. It won't be long until students have mastered this speed reading technique.

Lesson Eight

Skimming and Scanning

In the many years we have been working with secondary students, we have found few who have developed and perfected the skills of skimming and scanning. Skimming and scanning are extremely useful reading skills, but are not substitutes for a more careful study-type procedure for attaining complete comprehension in some subject areas.

Skimming and Scanning

Skimming is the most rapid of all reading rates, and the most complex. Relying on research results of the most recent eye-movement photography, we can be assured that reading faster than 800 to 900 words per minute is in truth "skimming." Skimming is not reading every word, sentence, or paragraph. Skimming is skipping with skilled judgment. The ability to skim with skilled judgment requires near perfect and instantaneous recognition of main ideas, transitional paragraphs, paragraphs describing key definitions or concepts, and summary paragraphs. A skimming facility requires initially superior reading skills. Without them, skimming becomes a random wandering through a word maze.

Scanning, on the other hand, involves running the eyes down the printed page, looking for specific bits of information, key words, or phrases. It is useful for locating statements, definitions, formulas, dates, telephone numbers, or other specific items which require little if any context. Whereas skimming is an organized search for seeking information about an article, chapter, or book, scanning is a hunt, skip-and-search technique for locating answers to specific questions. Scanning is useful for finding answers to simple questions and permits the eyes to move rapidly down the page searching for the answer. Once it's found, reading stops.

Search Reading

Since skimming is the fastest speed with which an individual covers printed material, obviously the reader is going to omit a great deal of the selection's content.

As such, it becomes the art of search reading, omitting everything else. We skim when searching for a phone number, a price in an advertisement, or a word in the dictionary. We do it when reading the headlines in the daily newspaper. Some readers do it when they want to see what is happening next in a mystery novel.

The skimming technique indeed is a useful study reading tool, for it is in this area that students will find its greatest utility. If students first look quickly over their assigned lessons, trying to get the main idea, and then go back and read carefully, they will more fully comprehend than if the material is read once slowly from beginning to end. Skimming is also useful for reviewing purposes whether it be a week or semester's work. Not only does it aid in completing classroom assignments, but it will speed up all of students' out-of-class supplementary reading assignments. Remind students that skimming is useful when writing themes and research papers. Much time will be lost if, when looking for specific information, students don't use a skimming technique.

Pointers

How does one go about learning to "read" at this extremely fast rate? It really isn't too difficult if students follow these few pointers. First, read the opening paragraph at the fastest average rate. This means that nothing will be left out, but it does get students started and involved in the idea of the selection, its setting, the author's style, and the story's mood. Often an author provides an introduction in the first few paragraphs, making available an overall picture of the content. But very quickly, students must begin leaving out much of the material. This is done by reading only the topic sentences of succeeding paragraphs, moving on to the last sentence in each paragraph. The eyes may even race down through the paragraph, picking up several important words or phrases. If the key sentence isn't the first sentence, then students may have to scan the paragraph to pick up the central thought or key phrases that describe the paragraph's main idea. Remind students that, when skimming, their only interest is in securing the main idea of every paragraph and a few supporting details and to do it in the shortest possible time.

Brain Control

Skimming for review is useful for recalling important facts or concepts students have already studied. It helps them zero in on the paragraph's purpose for being—its containment of a single important idea. As such, skimming provides a mental outline for review purposes by which most needed information is located for recall purposes.

There is no doubt about it, skimming is an exercise in brain control; it requires a mental set designed to read against time. To develop this skill effectively, students must try to read as fast as they can, at the same time omitting large chunks of material. It is a technique to use when students haven't much time, and when they need to cover the material in the shortest possible span. Of course, skimming requires practice, and in its early stages, comprehension will probably decrease as students' reading speed remains static. In time, however, and with daily practice, skimming rates will vastly improve.

Lesson Nine

Skimming for the Main Idea

Skimming Techniques

Skimming is always used for a specific purpose—a purpose to be clearly established in the students' minds so that they'll know what they're looking for. Perhaps two examples will clarify this statement. Ask students if they ever examined a painting and wondered what the artist was trying to say. In all probability, they have skimmed an artist's work and found little or nothing with which to identify. Lacking a point of reference, they were left in a vacuum. Or, ask students if they have ever inspected last year's school photograph of the football team, identified a player, and immediately recalled a startling pass reception in the homecoming game. In examining each picture, a skimming technique was used. In the painting, no central thought or theme was apparent. In the photograph, details were skipped and the eye zeroed in on the principal purpose of the inspection. In both cases, although purpose had been established, only in the latter was it completely satisfied.

Skimming for the main idea is much like skimming the photograph. A search was made for a reference point that ultimately led to the main idea. Details were of secondary importance. Thus, skimming for the main idea is a process of reading key sentences and ignoring everything else. What is read is read carefully so that all important facts may be tied together into a meaningful whole.

Main Idea

Skimming for the main idea is an extremely useful technique to use when students are previewing material, when they are reviewing material, or when they don't have enough time to do a thorough job. Any good paragraph, chapter, article, or book is organized in a logical manner. All good writers use an outline to organize their main ideas—those they want to convey to the reader. Once they establish and organize their ideas in a logical sequence, the ideas are developed in full. The key to skimming for main ideas lies in the reader's ability to detect, in advance, methods used to present these ideas. The clue to writers' method lies in their paragraph development. Some writers replace the paragraph's introductory sentence with a topic sentence. If this be the case, students should read the topic sentence, then skip the following paragraph and do the same. If the author places key ideas in the concluding sentence, then students should read that sentence. But there are writers who tend to place their main ideas in the middle of the paragraph. This arrangement requires a little more visual work on the part of the skimmer because a search must be made for significant words or phrases that lead to the main idea. There are still other writers who divide the key idea between the first and the last sentences of the paragraph. This format requires the reading of both sentences to obtain the central throught. Students should force themselves to ignore all sentences containing details. They are of less importance to the purpose. Once the paragraph pattern has been detected, students will have identified the key to skimming for main ideas.

Logical Sequence

As key sentences are read, students will quickly become aware of the logical sequence used by the writer in developing his or her thought. Should a gap appear in that logic, students will know they have missed a key sentence. If the train of thought is broken by that gap, they should glance quickly through the entire paragraph until they do locate the key sentence. If the key sentence can't be found, then what? The answer lies in a required search for key words. These are clue words usually contained in the key or topic sentence regardless of where it is found in the paragraph. Any student who really knows how to study will be able to quickly identify key words in text as evidenced by the fact that it is those words he or she underlines when studying.

Occasionally readers will find a rare author whose paragraphs consist of no key sentences. Instead, the writer presents material in groups of sentences having approximately the same value. All sentences contribute to the central theme and none stand alone. If students ever come in contact with this writing pattern, it is mandatory that they rely heavily on their mental assimilation skills because the main idea must be inferred! Fortunately, this type of literary construction is rare.

Typographical Details

Overall, and in conjunction with the suggestions just listed, students should be alert to typographical details—headings, subheadings, italics, and boldface print. Each of these skimming clues indicates important information. Students should note all transitional and number words, words like "in addition to," "moreover," "primary," "in the first place," and "finally." These words indicate relationships

Lesson Ten

Skimming for Details

Analogy

Read the following paragraph to the class:

You have just spent the weekend laboriously writing a required essay for Monday morning's literature class. Sunday night you gather your schoolbooks and assignments preparatory to catching tomorrow morning's bus. At this point, you make an earth-shaking discovery! Somehow, your essay has been mislaid! Where is it? Who took it? You must find it! With that single thought in mind, you search upstairs, downstairs, even in the basement. Everything is turned upside down in your bedroom. Old letters are thrown about, books are opened, wastebaskets are emptied, all the while a torrent of questions are asked. That one sheet of paper—your essay—is somewhere in the house! Skimming for details is much like your frantic search for that essay. It is a speedy search for a particular bit of information, and it must be found.

Details versus Main Ideas

In some school subjects, it is just as important to read for details as it is to read for main ideas. This is especially true when studying assignments in science and mathematics because of their precise and compact nature. The students' primary purpose is to study; skimming is not the technique to use. If they are reviewing, however, it is not only permissible, but is suggested that they skim.

What are details? Details are descriptive words, phrases, or sentences used to explain the central thought or main idea. As single words, details may appear as descriptive adjectives. As phrases, they provide a broader description of the main idea. As sentences, they furnish proof of the central thought. In the latter case, a word or phrase might be insufficient to prove the value of an important statement; additional details are of utmost importance. Often, one needs to find specific details concerning a certain topic. If this is the requirement, it isn't necessary to read all the material. All readers need to do is skim each paragraph until the paragraph is found that deals with the topic, then read that section carefully.

Categories

Realizing that details tend to support the main idea of a paragraph, we find that they fall into four categories, each of which is treated in the same manner: (1) a simple list which appears in no apparent order of importance; (2) chronological order in which events occur; (3) comparison-contrast where items are alike or different; and (4) cause-and-effect relationships. Once these classifications are recognized, it is a simple matter to apply a skimming technique.

Supporting Facts

When skimming for details, students should search for specific bits of information that contribute to main ideas. It may be a word in the dictionary, a topic listed in the index, a date in a history book, a name in the telephone directory, or a new word in the glossary. In each case, the search is for one specific informational item. Students should force themselves to disregard everything else until the particular item is found. Students should not let their minds wander; they should stick close to their purpose. When trained to skim effectively, students will find many opportunities to use this skill. Upon occasion, it is necessary to search for several supporting details, a situation common to many school assignments. An efficient reader first spots the main idea, then skims for supporting facts. A helpful device for use in these situations is borrowed from the newspaper world. A good reporter knows that supporting facts must provide the "who, what, when, where, and why" data. Students, too, can use these guideposts when skimming for details and skip the rest of the material.

Clues

Several other clues prove useful in identifying important details. Students should watch for numbering systems in the text such as "first," "second," and "third." Negative words such as "no," "not," and "neither" are powerful and should attract attention. So should the "how many" words; they, too, are significant clues. Such words as "none," "some," "always," and "more than half" usually indicate significant details. And, finally, students should look for and observe punctuation clues. Question marks, colons, semicolons, italics, and brackets all indicate important bits of information. Sometimes, however, important details are not set apart by any of the clues listed above. If that is the case, students must really concentrate on the word, fact, or bit of information they need. By concentrating on their need, the bit of required information will literally jump off the page when finally located.

Suggestion

Students should begin practice by skimming newspaper columns. They should skim for the five "w's." Then they should move on to wider columns and more difficult material. The more skimming they do—and do daily—the easier it will be to skim their assignments. They should be surprised by the great amount of information they can accumulate by skimming at rapid speeds. Remind them that an expert skimmer is a tenacious reader. They determine what they need and keep that purpose uppermost in their minds. By using skimming skills, they'll save themselves many reading hours every week.

Improve Your Speed in Social Studies

Basic Skills

Up to now, this book has been concerned with the development of several different rapid reading skills such as establishing reading purpose, previewing, reading in thought units, skimming for the main idea, and skimming for details. It makes no difference whether or not students are reading an assignment in social studies, mathematics, science, or literature; constant use should be made of these skills. In all probability, students won't be using all of these skills in reading a given assignment, but they will use combinations of several in reading different selections. An effective reader guarantees comprehension when he or she demonstrates competence in using these common and basic skills.

But competence in itself will not do the complete job. Something more is needed. The expert reader understands that the common speed reading skills are used in different ways in different subject areas. That is to say, although students are able to use the skills efficiently, these skills won't suffice completely unless students know *when* to use them. Certain special skills are required for reading different kinds of textual content. In other words, the expert reader doesn't read all subject area materials in the same manner. He or she must first identify the writing pattern used in a particular subject and then adjust his or her reading skill to the material's format. In the next few lessons, students will learn something about the nature and process of reading social studies, mathematics, science, and literature. Suggestions made will help them read more effectively in these areas. Now that students have learned to use the basic procedures for reading effectively, the additional "know-how" techniques of pursuing special subject material will complete the body of reading skills. After concluding this section, students should have no difficulty in reading any text effectively.

When reading social studies assignments, students should use all the basic speed reading skills discussed in preceding lessons. These include rapid reading, previewing, reading in thought units, skimming for main ideas, skimming for details, and utilizing that important first requirement: establishing their reading purpose. Not all skills will be used in every assignment, but students will use several skills in each reading selection.

Writing Patterns

First of all, examine the writing patterns of most social studies texts. Social studies content includes cause-and-effect material, events that are always sequenced, and an abundance of details, most of which are remote in time and place. Some social studies texts are more easily read because they are written in simple narrative style. Of particular importance is the problem of vocabulary. Because time and space are components of history and geography—evidenced by their ancient dates and faraway places—students have little personal experience or association with these concepts. Even when the vocabulary deals with modern institutions and events, concepts are likely to be complex and beyond immediate concern. Like science and mathematics, the social studies have their own "world of special vocabulary," a vocabulary that must be mastered. Surely the electoral college is not a university, nor is the presidential cabinet a regal piece of furniture.

Preview

The first thing students need to do when attacking a social studies assignment is to preview the chapter, noting its title and all headings. This establishes an overall perspective of the chapter's contents. Such practice permits students to identify the author's theme and general organizational pattern. As students preview, they should relate that perspective to facts and concepts previously studied. By doing so, they are recalling what they already know about the subject. Prepared with a good idea of what the writer is trying to say, students should skim the material. They should note major subheadings—usually boldface or italicized. If the chapters lack headings, students should skim the material page by page, keeping in mind their predetermined questions. Then they should skim for their answers. Remind students to keep on the lookout for all main points and supporting details. They should be alert for central ideas in paragraphs, and ignore those that are insignificant.

Review

Once the selection has been completed, students should recall all main points, supporting ideas, and important details. Finally, they should skim to make sure there are no serious omissions. Ask students to attack all succeeding sections or chapters in the same manner, and if necessary, review the material as a whole to grasp its overall perspective and organization.

Lesson Twelve

Improve Your Speed in Mathematics

Reading Math

For most students, whether they have taken courses in industrial arts, general mathematics, business arithmetic, algebra, or geometry, math remains an extremely difficult area. Reading skills are equally important in these areas. Just as specialized reading skills are required in other areas of study, several important skills in mathematics are worthy of note. Before proceeding further, consider a general view of the mathematics area.

Math Vocabularies

Reading in mathematics presents some very real problems for even the most efficient reader. For one thing, its vocabulary is more limited and exacting than that of any other area, with the possible exception of science. Mathematical vocabularies and symbols require a high degree of precision in their definitions. Sentences are short and to the point. A considerable number and type of thought processes are demanded and must be applied in logical sequence. Simple common words such as "compare," "by definition," and "therefore" require the severest form of critical perception. Reading rate must of necessity be slow; there can be no skimming. Every word, symbol, and phrase must be thoroughly weighed for its exact meaning. The efficient reader must continually ask the questions, "What does this really mean?", "Is this absolutely true in all cases?", and "Where do I go from here?" Because mathematics contains so much detailed reading-thinking involvement, it may be necessary to read the material several times to detect the problem's parameters or scope and ultimate solution.

Math Shorthand

Another difficulty is that mathematics is presented in a "shorthand" or symbolic language. Comprehension is difficult to achieve until precise meaning is given to all symbols. Because meaning is imperative, the reader may find it necessary to translate the symbolic language into one that is less obscure and more meaningful. To do this, students must check their understanding by restating the problem in their own words. Success in problem solving depends totally upon the students' thoroughness in accurately reading and understanding the problem. Without this degree of comprehension, it will be impossible for them to grasp the problem's orientation. Therefore, we suggest that students make it a point to discover the "givens," know what is wanted and needs to be done, assign appropriate values to each symbol, and then make the computation.

Students must take note of the fact that the language of mathematics is made up of three distinct types of symbols: (1) word symbols, (2) number symbols, and (3) letter symbols such as those used in algebra. The interpretation of this language makes for slow, methodical, and often extremely difficult analysis. Skipping an unfamiliar word or symbol quickly leads to miscalculation and failure.

Eye Movement

Another problem in reading mathematics is the change the reader must make in eye movement habits. Normally, when reading usual text, the eyes move in a single left-to-right directional pattern. In mathematics, however, not only do the eyes make vertical and horizontal movements, they must also be trained to zero in on the problem's specific details without overshooting the significant target. Often students waste considerable time because they are unable to focus their eyes on a specific symbol or detail in a problem.

Suggestions

Here are a few suggestions on how to read many math problems. First, students should read the entire problem to become acquainted with its component parts. They should concentrate on the problem's question. Often implied, it is the one that requires total attention and computational skills. Students should decide beforehand what methods, processes, or formulas are to be used. Then students should assemble all the facts and symbols required to complete the computation before they proceed. The reading done *before* the computation will in large part determine students' success or failure.

Remind students to learn to plot mentally their progress through a problem to a successful conclusion before beginning the computation. The process of reasoning requires ideas, concentration, and meaning. Reasoning itself means the rearranging or relating of elements to the point where "what is wanted" becomes the result of "what is known."

Improve Your Speed in Science

Background

Students who read reasonably well in most subject areas often have a great deal of difficulty in mastering science materials. It really isn't the fault of the reader; the problem rests in the manner in which science materials are written and developed. Science materials incorporate patterns of classification, detailed statements of fact, explanations of processes, interpretations of equations and reference tables, and a combination of the above. It is no wonder some students have difficulty in comprehending the complexities of scientific discovery and inquiry.

Moreover, students have become accustomed to the type of reading required when using classroom "readers" and library books. To date, most students' reading experiences and assignments have been primarily concerned with story plots, descriptions, and characterization. Content included in these books has been written in simple narrative, and paragraphs have been limited to a single brief theme or concept. In comparison, science materials utilize a language in which explanations are complex, compressed, and concise. Science texts contain no plots or simple descriptions of people and events. Instead, they are filled with strange symbols, diagrams, charts, and patterns seldom encountered outside the laboratory.

Scientific Vocabulary

With scientific materials students study the "why" of an enormous body of knowledge, a question requiring a very specific answer. To add to students' reading discomfort, scientific concepts use a vocabulary that evolves constantly. With the complexity of modern technology and discovery, one might conclude that scientific material can never be skimmed but must be read in a slow and thoughtful manner.

As with other subject area disciplines, science material requires the utilization of highly technical vocabulary. There are more scientific and technical terms used in the English language than there are in the total vocabularies of many other languages. New, specialized words are being born daily. In fact, since many other languages have not yet translated or been able to translate many English scientific words into local language, our vocabulary has been arbitrarily adopted without even changing the pronunciation. To add to its difficulty, many scientific words require a specific interpretation that is totally unlike that given in our general language. "Coke" is a common word to every student, but in science it is a product made from bituminous coal that has been treated in absence of air. Certainly, a "reducing agent" is not one who sells memberships in the nearest fitness gym, nor is an "emulsion" always an oily mass in suspension in a watery liquid. The reinterpretation of words of this sort indicates the importance of mastering the correct scientific vocabulary.

Classification Pattern

Look at the patterns and techniques used in writing material of a scientific nature. One of the most commonly used is the "classification" pattern. This is one in which scientists sort out and put together various processes, elements, animals, rocks, and plants known to have common characteristics yet differing from one another in certain respects. Usually the writer will describe significant likenesses and differences pertaining to a single category. To increase speed in reading the classification pattern, students should quickly identify its form so that they may understand its individual characteristics, then read to discover ways in which its components are alike and different.

Statement-of-Fact and Technical Process Patterns

If the material states detailed facts about the subject, students should identify the main idea, then check out the details belonging to each central concept. Statement-of-fact text is easily read and can be covered quickly. If the text explains a technical process, speed decreases considerably. Since the technical process pattern is one of the most difficult to read, students must make sure that they thoroughly understand each step. Sometimes the process development involves an interpretation of a diagram. If this is the case, students should study the diagram along with the text, making constant referrals between the two. Having completed their reading, students should explain the diagram to themselves without referring to the text. When they are successful, they should repeat the steps of the process without referring to the diagram.

Equations

Frequently, equations are also sprinkled throughout the text. When encountering an equation, students must make sure that they understand each symbol and its definition. An interpretation of tables requires that students interpret the data along with that of the text.

In conclusion, whatever the writer's pattern, students must be alert to the purpose of a selection, identify its characteristics, then adjust their reading approaches to those criteria. In analyzing an efficient science reader's techniques, we find that he or she uses certain specific skills. An expert reader is able to identify general truths and draw accurate but specific conclusions from stated facts. He or she is able to apply previously learned knowledge to new problems and visualize relationships in logical sequence. The importance of ideas and concepts is readily grasped, and directions are accurately followed. Graphs, charts, and diagrams are comfortably interpreted. The scientific reader also exhibits a mastery of sorting out ideas and principles in ordered sequential patterns.

Name _____

Date _____

WARM-UP

INTERPRETATION EXERCISE

Time limit: 23 seconds

Directions: Check each item that cannot be tasted, seen, or heard.

_____ 1. worry and anxiety

_____ 2. concrete mixture

_____ 3. high morale

_____ 4. speedway races

_____ 5. double entry

_____ 6. juvenile delinquent

_____ 7. burning lamp

_____ 8. competitive cougars

_____ 9. hidden frustration

_____ 10. combined wheat

_____ 11. ghost of a chance

_____ 12. swimming algae

_____ 13. continuing displeasure

_____ 14. subtle tears

_____ 15. doubloons

_____ 16. patient attitude

_____ 17. conceived in liberty

_____ 18. current smog

_____ 19. facsimile

_____ 20. living standard

Time _____   *Errors* _____   *Score* _____

99

PERCEPTION EXERCISE

Time limit: 28 seconds

Directions: Underline the same word as the key word.

Key Word

 1. thunder — sounder, thicken, asunder, blunder, thunder
 2. scream — cream, screech, screen, scream, ream
 3. though — through, throe, though, thought, throw
 4. tartly — tardy, tartly, hearty, hardy, tort
 5. bicycle — cycle, tricycle, unicycle, bicycle, codicil
 6. youth — truth, sooth, young, youth, your, booth
 7. wicket — wicket, wished, wicked, washed, twisted
 8. season — reason, season, treason, erosion, session
 9. refuse — regain, renew, refuse, renege, regular
10. tingle — triple, tipple, tickle, tingle, tangle
11. swell — swill, swallow, dwell, swell, still
12. stipple — tipple, steeple, steel, people, stipple
13. wretch — wrench, witch, writ, wretch, watch
14. slippery — slipper, stopper, slipping, slip sheet, slippery
15. herself — shelf, selfish, myself, himself, herself
16. breathe — breath, wreath, wreak, breach, breathe, earth
17. jade — jag, jaded, jaywalk, Jake, fade, jade
18. acquire — admire, retire, lyre, acquire, require, mire
19. barker — barber, harken, barker, border, barely
20. lathe — bathe, lathe, tithe, bather, lather

Time _____   Errors _____   Score _____

         Speed Reading for Better Grades

COMPREHENSION EXERCISE

Time limit: 38 seconds

Directions: Underline the word or words that mean the same or about the same as the key word.

Key Word

1. abide	pardon, candy, lawyer, continue in a place
2. eagerly	zealously, dart, needle, reckless one, nearly
3. gallant	terror, stately, pasture, savage criminal, gall
4. identical	vein, ghost, satisfaction, the same, dental
5. laborer	acquire, impression, one who works, thoroughly
6. quest	basis, seeking, verse, capactiy of barrel, guest
7. abundant	overflowing, lawn, affection, deceive more, bounded
8. fatigue	candle, weariness, capable, election, fate, fatty
9. garrison	darling, manager, soldiers at fort, feast, garage
10. nigh	faithful, near, decay, glitter, neigh, nightly
11. obvious	haste, olive, easily discovered, heap of clothing
12. sauce	import, partner, elder, income bracket, condiment
13. zone	laughter, venture, glimpse, belt, tone, cone
14. accuse	male, bring charges, incline, last, operate, action
15. feeble	physically weak, advise, marble, feet, feed often
16. genuine	parlor, weed, actual, refer, genus, genuflect
17. imperial	velvet, canoe, neglect, majestic, impose often
18. margin	wedding, border, opera, scare, marine, Marne
19. aboard	administrative, gleam, on a boat, thrill, lumber
20. earnest	important, not trivial, victim, heard, earned

Time _____   *Errors* _____   *Score* _____

Speed Reading for Better Grades

STORY I

Nearly three quarters of our earth's surface is covered by water, and the Pacific Ocean, by far the largest of the oceans, accounts for almost half of all the water area in the world. This vast ocean is twice as big as the Atlantic and more than 20 times as big as the United States. Furthermore, it is a good deal larger than all the land surfaces of the earth put together. The distance across its widest part, between Panama and the coast of Malaysia, is 11,000 miles, or about halfway around the earth.

The Pacific is also the deepest of the oceans with an average depth of nearly three miles. There are shallow parts, of course, some of which are occupied by many islands, large and small. On the other hand, near some of the chains of islands and near parts of the shore of Asia, great trenches are found in the ocean bottom that are tremendously deep. Northeast of the Philippines, for example, there is a spot 35,400 feet deep. In this spot the highest mountain on earth would lie with its peak more than a mile below the water's surface. All places more that 18,000 feet in depth are known as "deeps." The Pacific Ocean has 33 of these, the Atlantic 19, and the Indian Ocean only 5. Great size and depth combine to give the Pacific a volume of water that is between five and six times the volume of all the earth's land that lies above sea level. The average height above sea level of all the land is only half a mile; the average depth of the oceans as a whole is about 2½ miles.

1. The best title for this selection is (a) "Oceania," (b) "Facts and Figures," (c) "The Great Pacific," (d) "How Deep Is the Ocean?"

2. The earth's land surface compared with its water surface is (a) greater, (b) smaller, (c) the same, (d) not stated.

3. Rank the oceans in area: (a) Atlantic, Pacific, Indian, (b) Pacific, Indian, Atlantic, (c) Pacific, Atlantic, Indian, (d) not stated.

4. The widest part of the Pacific is near (a) the equator, (b) the far north, (c) the United States, (d) the Antarctic.

5. The average depth of the Pacific is (a) about 6½ miles, (b) about 3½ miles, (c) nearly 4 miles, (d) nearly 3 miles.

6. A "deep" must be at least (a) 18,000 feet, (b) 3 miles, (c) 35,400 feet, (d) unmeasureable.

7. Compared with all oceans, the Pacific's average depth is (a) smaller, (b) greater, (c) the same, (d) less than any other ocean.

8. In number of deeps, the Atlantic has (a) 5, (b) 33, (c) none, (d) 19.

9. The greatest depth mentioned is (a) 5 miles, (b) 4 miles, (c) 6.7 miles, (d) both b and c.

10. The deepest portion of the Pacific is located near (a) Malaysia, (b) Panama, (c) the United States, (d) the Philippines.

STORY II

What do hands, carats, and months have in common? They are all units of measurement based on the natural world. Weights and measures were among the earliest tools invented by humans. Understandably, primitive societies first turned to parts of the body and natural surroundings for measuring devices. Early Babylonian and Egyptian records indicate that length was measured with the forearm, hand, and finger. Though rarely used today, a hand is equal to four inches. In order to barter for food and raw materials, people filled containers such as gourds with plant seeds, which were then counted to measure the volume. The carat, now used to measure gold and diamonds, was originally equal to the weight of a seed from the carob tree. Months and years, based on the movements of the sun and moon, helped keep track of agricultural seasons and religious holidays.

As societies developed, weights and measures became more complex. The invention of numbering systems and the science of mathematics made it possible to create whole new systems of weights and measures appropriate to trade, commerce, land division, and later, scientific research. These measures had their origin in a variety of cultures and were difficult to relate between nations. Recognizing this need, Gabriel Mouton, vicar of St. Paul in Lyons, proposed in 1670 a comprehensive measuring system based on the length of one minute of an arc of the great circle of the earth, the metron. In 1790, the National Assembly of France requested the French Academy of Sciences to "deduce an invariable standard for all the measures and weights." Thus, the metric system was devised, introducing grams, kilometers, liters, and hectares.

1. The following is not given as an example of measurement: (a) kilometer, (b) carat, (c) decibel, (d) minute.

2. A hand is equal to (a) 12 inches, (b) 4 inches, (c) 6 inches, (d) 5 fingers.

3. Volume was first measured by (a) weighing water, (b) guessing, (c) counting seeds, (d) weighing stones.

4. The carat was derived from the weight of a (a) diamond, (b) carob seed, (c) mustard seed, (d) gourd.

5. An early device to measure time was the (a) calendar, (b) clock, (c) moon, (d) metron.

6. The development of a whole new system of weights and measures was aided by (a) early Babylonian records, (b) clay and metal vessels, (c) heavenly bodies, (d) the science of mathematics.

7. Before 1790, the major difficulty with the measuring systems of the world was that they were all (a) alike, (b) too comprehensive, (c) based on the earth, (d) different.

8. The metron is based on (a) the moon, (b) stones, (c) church history, (d) part of the great circle of the earth.

9. The person responsible for developing a measuring system that could be standardized was (a) Mouton, (b) St. Paul, (c) France, (d) Lyons.

10. The metric system was established in (a) 1970, (b) 1670, (c) 700 B.C., (d) 1790.

GWPM _____ *(times) Avg. Comp.* _____ *(equals) EWPM* _____

Lesson Fourteen

Improve Your Speed in Literature

Background

People read literature for appreciation and enjoyment and for a truly pleasurable experience. Reading literature is quite different from reading a selection in science, mathematics, or social studies. Reading purposes differ; we read with different attitudes, and we use quite different approaches. As a result, reading literature calls for several adjustments. While literature embraces a great variety of scopes, styles, patterns, forms, and subject matter, it also suggests possible problems in reading technique. Several procedures suggested in earlier lessons must necessarily be modified to accommodate varying writer styles and patterns. With these observations in mind, we'll examine several special skills appropriate to reading literature effectively.

Short Stories

Short stories seem to have a set of characteristic qualities that are singular to their style. The narrative contains a central theme that tells a story developed through a series of events leading to a climax. Basic to the short story is its element of emotion about a conflict, struggle, or problem. The writer's intent is to involve the reader actively in this mood.

Since there are different types of short stories written for differing purposes, the first thing readers must do is discover the purpose the writer had in mind when developing the theme. Once this has been identified, students should read along with the writer, noting each incident; students should respond to the writer's emotions, anticipate the struggle, and relax in the inevitable conclusion. If the short story is written in dialect, readers should attempt to identify with the writer's style and pattern, for it is the dialect that provides the locale's flavor and sense of authenticity. Should students have difficulty in reading dialect silently, suggest that they read it aloud until it becomes easier to follow. In doing this, many unusual spellings can be made comprehensible simply by the way they sound to the ear. Remind students to take their time; short stories are to be enjoyed. Because they are short, students must use their imaginations to fill in obvious omissions with their own ideas, making sure the additions do not violate any of the given facts or conditions. Students should analyze possible solutions and anticipate the conclusion. In other words, students should live the story as though they were really there!

Novels

Novels are distinguished from short stories by their length, number of characters, complicated plots and subplots, and descriptive passages. They require considerable reader interpretation, stress plot development (often through extensive conversational text) and require the development of a sensitivity to descriptive passages. Many novels include patterns of dialect, allusions, and figurative text. If some of these skills have eluded students, then the best way to achieve mastery is to read, and read some more. The reader is required to follow the novelist's plot and, if the novel is historical, identify with the period in which the characters lived. Authors aid the reader in this identification through descriptions, speeches, and dialogue. The reader is often asked to make inferences, pass judgments, and draw conclusions. To receive the greatest enjoyment, students should read each novel according to its pattern of presentation and execution. Adjusting attitudes, values, and reading skills to the author's intent affords a satisfactory experience for the reader.

Drama

Drama is often more difficult to read than other forms of literature because plot is developed through conversation. Unlike traditional paragraph patterns, dramatic literature uses brackets to describe scenes, give clues, and explain action. Often much of the play is printed in italic form. Because of these characteristics, special reading adjustments are required. Since each paragraph begins with a new speech—and many of them are quite brief—the eyes must accommodate themselves to differing indentations of the text. Many speeches in dramatic literature are open-ended; that is, they end in an irregular manner, thus leaving many unfilled lines. These unfilled lines require continuous eye-movement adjustments for following marginal cues. Another characteristic is the use of a different typeface to identity names of characters. No doubt, these typographical patterns require some adjustment and practice on the part of the reader. However, if students read plays regularly, their eyes will eventually adjust to the format.

Essays

Essays, according to the dictionary, are analytic or interpretative literary compositions dealing with a subject of more or less limited viewpoint. This means, then, that the reader is limited to the subject matter itself and the author's viewpoint. If students have little or no background in the subject, they may be unwilling to pursue the writer's interest. Students should decide whether or not they have similar interests; then read for information. For reading essays, reading speed will be quite slow because of their high literary style and intellectual persuasion.

Poetry

Poetry must be read quite differently from prose fiction, short stories, drama, or essays. As with other literary forms, poetry has its own peculiar characteristics. The most significant is in its conclusion—to say as much as possible in as few words as possible. Therefore, students must watch for what is suggested as well as what is stated. Furthermore, poetry is written to be heard; that is, it has ear appeal. Consequently, poetry should be read orally. Designed to give an imaginative impression to the ear, poetry utilizes similes and metaphors to appeal to the reader's senses. Figures of speech abound; rhythm and rhyme provide lyrical sequence. As such, poetry stirs the imagination and appeals to the emotions. Remind students to sit back, read slowly, and enjoy.

WARM-UP

INTERPRETATION EXERCISE   *Time limit: 22 seconds*

Directions: Check each item that can be classified as mineral, vegetable, or animal.

_____ 1. beefed about it

_____ 2. Siamese feline

_____ 3. frontier movement

_____ 4. St.-John's-wort

_____ 5. shocking time

_____ 6. cold shivers

_____ 7. read rapidly

_____ 8. maize

_____ 9. breaking dawn

_____ 10. diamond stud

_____ 11. graphite

_____ 12. no substitutions

_____ 13. timidity

_____ 14. lengthy discourse

_____ 15. first inkling

_____ 16. knobby pine

_____ 17. hamstrung

_____ 18. sudden shock

_____ 19. flaxen fabric

_____ 20. salty brine

Time _____   *Errors* _____   *Score* _____

PERCEPTION EXERCISE   *Time limit: 27 seconds*

Directions: Underline the same word as the key word.

Key Word

1. trite	trick, trite, recite, incite, decide, tripe
2. media	mediate, middle, muddle, media, medium, medial
3. corroborate	correlate, collar, corroborate, correct, corona
4. conscription	description, irrigation, conscription, ascribe
5. traction	attract, distract, contract, trick, traction
6. stupid	studied, stupid, student, stood, tepid
7. affront	confront, afford, affront, affect, affection
8. integrate	integrate, integral, disintegrate, interval, gate
9. presume	preclude, presumptuous, presume, produce, sum
10. laboratory	libel, liable, laboratory, labor, story
11. monitor	mentor, monitored, admonish, monitor, mother
12. boiled	soiled, boiled, spoiled, foiled, coiled
13. relation	population, relative, relation, nation, rely
14. contaminate	conception, contaminate, contain, retain, tan
15. recede	exceed, receive, recede, succeed, receipt
16. installation	install, installed, instill, installation, stall
17. precautions	precaution, interfere, propose, precautions
18. manufacture	manual, maple, manufacture, male, mania
19. inscription	inscribe, scribble, script, inscription
20. fission	fission, fishing, admission, fusion, hissing

Time _____   *Errors* _____   *Score* _____

                   Speed Reading for Better Grades

COMPREHENSION EXERCISE

Time limit: 37 seconds

Directions: Underline the word or words that mean the same or about the same as the key word.

Key Word

1.	absorb	scold, take in, unit, youthful, adore, ascorbic
2.	economy	thrifty management, temporary, warrant
3.	faculty	decrease, carpet, ability to do, faces, facility
4.	ignorant	elaborate, fiery, glare, carbon, obtuse, plug
5.	lame	mast, disabled foot, impress, easily, blameless
6.	panic	abundance, learning, banker, sudden fright, pans
7.	accord	calmly, grant, daylight, edition, corded tire
8.	barren	fatal, jealous, without offspring, landscape
9.	effective	able to produce, nephew, observer, pant, effect
10.	immense	rarely, salute, satisfaction, huge, tenseness
11.	jest	tank, undoubtedly, taunt, accordingly, justice
12.	lash	basin, bind with a cord, dear one, fee, leash
13.	mantle	genuine, hardness, immortal, loose overgarment
14.	parcel	manufacture, oral, portion, parliamentary act
15.	reality	being real, realm, scent, screw, drilling rig
16.	temporary	tempt, for a short time, unlike anything, wealth
17.	unit	achievement, bearer, single thing, cart, unite
18.	warrant	decree, security, elbow, glide, errand boy, war
19.	elaborate	hatch, impulse, lecture, detailed, labor party
20.	furious	mechanical, accustom, violent, bade, fiery party

Time _____   *Errors* _____   *Score* _____

STORY I

A letter from Russian novelist, poet, and literary scholar Vladimir Nabokov (author of *Lolita*) to his friend and literary colleague Edmund Wilson:

January 9, 1941

Dear Wilson,

A big *spaseebo* for "contacting" me with *Decision* and "New Direction[s]." I had a very pleasant talk with Klaus Mann who suggested my writing for them an article of 2,000 words. I got a letter from James Laughlin and am sending him my English novel *The Real Life of Sebastian Knight* which I retrieved from my agent. (I should have loved your reading it if I had a spare copy and you time.) Laughlin has also written me about a collection of modern Russian poems—particularly Pasternak (a first-class poet—do you know his stuff?).

I have been reading at the library all the monthlies for the Soviet year 1940,—a ghastly and very amusing task. This week my article for the *New Republic* (for which I have no more of that warm feeling since you have gone,—that stimulating warmth) will be ready. I am working hard at my lectures. In March I have got a fortnight of them at Wellesley Coll[ege] and yesterday I came back from Wells Coll[ege] where, to put it modestly, I had some success. Nicholas was charming.

When shall I see you?

My best regards to your wife and a good Russian handshake for you.

Yours truly,
V. Nabokov

[My wife sends both of you her cordial regards.]

1. We may infer that *spaseebo* means (a) contacting, (b) spaghetti, (c) thank you, (d) hello.
2. Klaus Mann asked Nabokov to write an article (a) about poetry, (b) about Russia, (c) of 2,000 words, (d) for the *New Republic*.
3. Nabokov had written a novel in English called (a) *Decision*, (b) *The Real Life of Sebastian Knight*, (c) *Klaus Mann*, (d) *Move Over, Lolita*.
4. Nabokov thinks that Pasternak is (a) a beatnik, (b) a scientist, (c) an agent, (d) a first-class poet.
5. We may infer that "monthlies" are (a) records, (b) accounting ledgers, (c) magazines, (d) libraries.
6. Nabokov had read a year's worth of Soviet journals, and he was (a) angry, (b) sad, (c) amused, (d) tired.
7. About the *New Republic*, Nabokov said that he no longer felt that stimulating (a) reading, (b) challenge, (c) readership, (d) warmth.
8. Nabokov said he would be giving lectures at Wellesley for two (a) days, (b) weeks, (c) months, (d) years.
9. At Wells College, Nabokov felt that he was (a) underpaid, (b) successful, (c) ineffective, (d) avoided.
10. Nabokov sends his regards to Wilson and his (a) son, (b) wife, (c) daughter, (d) brother.

STORY II

Each season, gardeners, vacationers, and recreation buffs empty the contents of gasoline cans into power mowers, garden tools, motorboats, camp stoves, and snowmobiles. Underwriters Laboratories reveals that thousands of people each year seek hospital treatment for injuries associated with liquid fuels. Fires and explosions are the chief hazards associated with improper use of gasoline. The following suggestions for gasoline use and storage are offered:

1. Use a safety can for storage—one with a pouring spout and a tight-fitting cap or valve. Vapors must be vented to relieve pressure buildup in the can.
2. Never use a glass jar or makeshift container for storage. Use a safety can with a safe and convenient carrying handle.
3. Do not store gasoline in a car or car trunk. Vapors may filter into the car's interior where ignition sources exist. A rear-end collision (even a minor one) may cause an explosion.
4. Never use gasoline for cleaning clothes or paintbrushes, for exterminating insects, or for starting fires.
5. Do not syphon gasoline by mouth. If it gets into your lungs, a few drops can kill you.

Remember that gasoline is extremely flammable and can readily explode when it vaporizes in the air in the presence of an ignition source.

1. Accidents involving gasoline occur during (a) summer, (b) spring, (c) all seasons, (d) winter.
2. The following is *not* listed as a user of gasoline: (a) gardener, (b) vacationer, (c) drag racer, (d) recreation buff.
3. The primary dangers of improper use are (a) damage to lungs and death, (b) rear-end collision and fire, (c) fire and explosion, (d) poisonous fumes and explosion.
4. Gasoline should be stored in (a) a glass jar, (b) a safety can, (c) a plastic container, (d) a garage.
5. One should not store gasoline in a car trunk because (a) pressure builds up, (b) gasoline gets into the lungs, (c) gasoline kills insects, (d) there could be an explosion due to collision.
6. One example of an "ignition source" is (a) a paintbrush, (b) a match, (c) a safety can, (d) vaporization.
7. A proper use of gasoline is as (a) a starter for the fireplace, (b) a cleaning fluid, (c) an insect killer, (d) fuel for a mower.
8. A danger associated with syphoning gasoline is (a) vaporizing in the air, (b) igniting clothes, (c) getting gasoline in the lungs, (d) exploding in the mouth.
9. Liquid fuel causes injuries that number in the (a) none, (b) teens, (c) hundreds, (d) thousands.
10. The best way to store gasoline in a car is (a) in the trunk, (b) not at all, (c) in a safety can, (d) in the back seat.

GWPM _____ *(times) Avg. Comp.* _____ *(equals) EWPM* _____

Study-Reading and Memory

Background

Many secondary students confuse reading with studying, and even though 90 percent of material learned at this level is derived from reading, the processes are not identical. Of course it's correct to say that studying usually involves reading, but if the individual is doing nothing more than reading words, he is not practicing study-reading. Nor is study-reading solely reserved for students, assignments, or examinations. Most people study a variety of printed materials. Chefs study cookbooks, accountants study the income tax form, bankers study their financial pages, and farmers study agricultural publications. We all, in varying degrees, study something every day whether it be a set of instructions, theory, or general information. This lesson is devoted to the development of study-reading skills and the improvement of memory.

Memory Improvement

The study skills that follow are not concerned with describing different ways of reading but instead with the application of students' already mastered skills. As such, they apply to study activities emphasizing the improvement of recall and memory. Although reading is an important part of most study activity, it is not the entire process. Researchers conducted experiments where study techniques were compared with ordinary reading and found that students who used the following study technique came out ahead of those who simply read and reread a given assignment. Study-reading, unlike general reading, requires an organized approach to the task. Unlike recreational reading (which requires no predetermined plan of action), study-reading requires the ability to select needed information, understand it quickly, commit this information to memory for immediate and delayed recall, and finally, review the studied material satisfactorily.

P-Q-R-S-T

During World War II, the Armed Forces devised an efficient and proven study-reading method for use in all their training programs. Based on the findings of psychological research, this method, when properly applied, is guaranteed to improve students' effectiveness in study-reading. Using it, students might even find themselves on the honor roll. But the plan must be conscientiously carried out. Named the P-Q-R-S-T study method, its symbols are easily remembered because the letters and their activities are in alphabetical and consecutive order:

PREVIEW ▶ QUESTION ▶ READ ▶ STATE ▶ TEST

Preview: Students should skim through the reading material, turning the pages rapidly. They should glance at all headings, subheadings, and introductory and concluding paragraphs. Ask students to skim topic sentences, searching for the general theme of each paragraph. These procedures provide an overall perspective of the assignment. But students shouldn't spend too much time doing this. It takes only a few minutes.

Question: Students should skim the section or chapter asking themselves questions about what they have seen. They should turn all headings and subheadings into questions. Students should ask themselves the "who, what, when, where, and why" questions and be sure to find the answers. If there are no subheadings, students should skim the material anyway. The idea is to get the central theme of the material. Base your questions on and relate them to these central themes. By questioning, you are laying the foundation for purposeful reading, reading that provides answers. By following these steps, you are beginning to *think* about the selection's content instead of reading blindly.

Read: Students should now read the material in such a manner that their questions will be fully answered. Attempting to answer previously developed mental questions opens the door to higher levels of comprehension and true study. So far, students have gained an idea of what the central idea is and, more importantly, established a genuine and fundamental purpose for study. Because of their awareness that certain questions must be answered, levels of concentration increase—students know they're looking for something special. Through increased interest, students will have a good feeling when they come across an answer.

State: Students stating what they have read is nothing more than old-fashioned oral recitation. If they are studying with someone, students tell (state) him or her what they have learned. If they study alone, students should review their questions and write down their answers. If it helps to talk, then students should talk to themselves. The point is, students should involve as many sense organs as possible in their stating process (speech, hearing, writing).

Test: After a few days, ask students to review the material and test their recall. Psychologists tell us that the period of most forgetting is immediately after learning. That's why students should wait a few days. Periodic review reinforces and improves retention and recall. The "test" step is an important phase of the study-reading process.

Review with students what they have learned about improving study-reading skills. By utilizing this study plan, students have prepared themselves for serious concentration of the assignment. They're now reading with a purpose that provides a sense of direction. Preview and skimming skills are being used to identify main ideas—they also help keep students' minds from wandering. Other reading skills are being actively employed, such as identifying details, paragraph patterns, and transitional paragraphs. Comprehension is being reinforced and recall sharpened by review. Together, these skills and techniques afford a most promising avenue to greatly improved reading proficiency.

WARM-UP

INTERPRETATION EXERCISE

Time limit: 21 seconds

Directions: Check each item that has been manufactured.

_____ 1. pleasurable conquest	_____ 11. meteorite
_____ 2. late-model conveyance	_____ 12. my English teacher
_____ 3. forest timber	_____ 13. dehydrated milk
_____ 4. geological formation	_____ 14. hay fever
_____ 5. aspirin tablets	_____ 15. duck-billed platypus
_____ 6. natural habitat	_____ 16. mountaintop
_____ 7. skirting the woods	_____ 17. fat-free
_____ 8. student's notebook	_____ 18. surface tension
_____ 9. sheared shrubbery	_____ 19. bone china
_____ 10. hard cash	_____ 20. conquered territory

Time _____   *Errors* _____   *Score* _____

PERCEPTION EXERCISE

Time limit: 26 seconds

Directions: Underline the same word as the key word.

Key Word

1.	reactor	react, reactor, detract, retreat, traction
2.	uranium	radium, aquarium, plutonium, uranium
3.	annoyed	destroyed, defrayed, annoyed, noise, boy
4.	tribal	trouble, triple, tremble, tribal, treble
5.	agronomy	astronomy, aground, agreeable, agronomy, again
6.	elementary	elemental, elephant, subsequent, elementary
7.	antiques	techniques, oblique, antics, antiques, article
8.	mythical	mystical, myth, mythical, ethical, icicle
9.	physiology	philosophy, physiology, psychology, cyclone
10.	cultural	cultural, culture, cultivate, convent, coupler
11.	multiply	multiplication, masticate, multiply, follicle
12.	engine	engineer, ending, engineered, engine, Indian
13.	froth	forth, forty, froth, fourth, firth
15.	hurrah	hurry, hurrah, Harry, hairy, surrey
15.	jackal	jackal, jacket, packet, jaguar, cackle
16.	frighten	freight, frighten, heighten, tighten, fright
17.	kernel	kennel, kettle, kernel, knuckle, kneed
18.	sadden	sudden, saddle, supply, sadden, setting
19.	tiptoe	toes, tipsy, topping, tipper, tiptoe
20.	spinach	spanning, spinach, spun, spin ache, spout

Time _____   *Errors* _____   *Score* _____

© 1978, 1998 J. Weston Walch, Publisher   *116*

COMPREHENSION EXERCISE

Time limit: 36 seconds

Directions: Underline the word or words that mean the same or about the same as the key word.

Key Word

1. facility	educate, ease of doing, guilty, face
2. ignorance	favorable, youngster, without knowledge, barren
3. naval	gasp, ache, vessels of war, death, novel, stores
4. objection	hardship, bounty, expression of disagreement, economy, effective date
5. quiver	illustration, battery, shake, fearful, quitter
6. talent	superior ability, captive, faculty, geese, tall one
7. wail	jersey, captive, mournful sound, finery, vale
8. abuse	kneel, improper treatment, gallop, immense, buses
9. baron	lark, decoration, title, jest, barren hillside
10. educate	management, develop knowledge, ignorant, knot
11. gasp	nineteen, fierce, jail, catch one's breath, gas
12. illustration	picture, gesture, lame, lash, lusty, straight
13. reaction	obviously, opposing action, maintain, maintained
14. unfortunate	parallel, impose, unsuccessful, ninety, fortune
15. ache	reaction, suffer pain, neat, occasional, take
16. battery	scare, jolly, obligation, unlawful beating, water
17. captive	a prisoner, leaf, panic, parcel, captain, carport
18. fiercely	telegraph, marvel, violently, reality, farce, pirate
19. impose	unfortunate, absorb, undertake, force on others, repose
20. marvel	warmth, causing wonder, waiting scarlet, mortal

Time _____   *Errors* _____   *Score* _____

STORY I

Ever since Samuel Morse had demonstrated his invention of the telegraph to the American Congress in 1844, wealthy Cyrus Field had been dreaming of the day he might set up a transatlantic wire service. He was not to know that once begun it would take a dozen years and considerable heartache. In surveying the needs for such a venture, Field was confronted with a multitude of problems. He needed an extremely sensitive device for receiving electrical signals over long distances of cables. Lord Kelvin provided him with the mirror galvanometer. Thousands of miles of strong, flexible cable had to be manufactured. Insulated with gutta-percha, the cable had to be bound with brass to protect it from marine borers. Ships had to be redesigned to carry the enormous reels of wire, and machinery had to be designed to pay out the cable smoothly. Should the cable break, some grappling system had to be devised to recover the loose end. At last, in August, 1858, after one unsuccessful attempt the previous year, the operation was completed and the first transatlantic message was sent. Two months later, insulation problems wrought havoc with the cable and fresh a start had to be made.

Seven years later, another attempt to lay a new cable was made, only to lose it two thirds of the way across the Atlantic. At last, on July 28, 1866, all obstacles were overcome with the cable permanently established. Queen Victoria was the first person to use the new cable, sending a greeting to President Andrew Johnson.

1. The initial transatlantic message by cable was completed in (a) 1844, (b) 1866, (c) 1858, (d) 1892.

2. The builder of the first Atlantic cable system was (a) Cypress, (b) Kelvin, (c) Queen Victoria, (d) Field.

3. The construction job was (a) comparatively easy, (b) a snap, (c) without incident, (d) difficult.

4. A mirror galvanometer (a) makes sparks, (b) sends code, (c) receives electrical impulses, (d) designs transmissions.

5. Lord Kelvin was probably (a) French, (b) English, (c) American, (d) none of these.

6. Brass protected the cable from (a) thieves, (b) sea water, (c) marine life, (d) whales.

7. Gutta-percha was used as (a) a strengthening agent, (b) an insulator, (c) a stiffener, (d) not stated.

8. When the cable broke, the end was retrieved (a) by diving, (b) by frogmen, (c) with grappling hooks, (d) by no one.

9. Once permanently established, the first cable communication originated (a) in the United States, (b) overland, (c) in England, (d) on the Atlantic.

10. Prior to the first transmission, (a) one, (b) two, (c) three, (d) four unsuccessful attempts had been made.

STORY II

It was a tense meeting of the city commissioners. The room was silent. Suddenly, the silence was broken by a voice. "Call your home immediately." No one was more startled than an assistant city manager. She quickly pushed the button on the tiny, wallet-sized gadget hooked on her briefcase. It was her beeper that had dented the silence.

This modern-age electronic device—technically known as a radio-pager—keeps tens of thousands of people in touch with their home bases. Most beepers just beep, signaling that the carrier should call for a message, but newer models talk. Regardless of the response, their insistent sound has joined other dominant sounds of our civilization, such as squealing tires, Muzak™, and packed mufflers. Are these gadgets really new? Doctors, newspaper people, and mechanics have been using them since 1950 to keep in touch with their patients, bosses, or clients. But the great increase in their popularity came during the energy crisis. Many companies found it more efficient to get pagers so they could keep sales- or service-people moving without expending extra fuel. Before the 1970's, the beepers required a go-between. A call went to an answering service where a human being punced a button to activate the beep. Now a computer activates the beeper's own seven-digit phone number. When it's dialed, the person calling will hear a busy signal, then a beep, indicating the beeper has been set off. In more sophisticated models, it means "Go ahead and talk."

1. The major topic of this story is (a) city commissioners, (b) noise, (c) telephones, (d) radio-pagers.
2. The purpose of the "beeper" is to (a) break up meetings, (b) serve as a phone, (c) start a computer, (d) signal a call.
3. One event that increased the popularity of "beepers" was (a) a meeting of city commissioners, (b) the energy crisis, (c) a strike of the phone company, (d) a conference of doctors.
4. The model owned by the assistant manager was (a) wallet-sized, (b) briefcase-sized, (c) button-sized, (d) television-sized.
5. Recent models have replaced human go-betweens with a (a) telephone, (b) computer, (c) radio, (d) button.
6. One group *not* listed as a user in the 1950's is (a) physicians, (b) mechanics, (c) newswriters, (d) computer sales agents.
7. The earliest beepers were activated by (a) a phone number, (b) a person, (c) a client, (d) an electronic device.
8. A dominant sound of our civilization *not* listed in this selection is (a) beepers, (b) tires, (c) mufflers, (d) airplanes.
9. The first thing that a person hears when calling is (a) a beep, (b) the voice of the person calling, (c) a busy signal, (d) squealing.
10. According to the story, most models (a) beep and talk, (b) beep and record, (c) beep only, (d) keep salespeople moving.

GWPM _____ *(times) Avg. Comp.* _____ *(equals) EWPM* _____

Lesson Sixteen

Teacher Page

Continuing Progress Through Practice

A Lifetime Process

It is hoped that this introduction to an important communication skill will spur students on to greater accomplishment. They have been introduced to and hopefully mastered the skills of previewing and reading in thought units; they have learned the importance of establishing reading purpose, how to skim, how to develop a comprehensive vocabulary, and received instructions for improving memory and recall. As with any skill, increased proficiency results from continuous practice. We suggest, therefore, that students use these skills daily and apply them consistently, remembering that the improvement of reading is not a one-time thing—it is indeed a lifetime process. As such, optimum achievement levels are seldom realized.

In studying the daily lessons, students have learned that reading is a complex process. Each student, according to their differing backgrounds and training, meets the printed page differently with varying degrees of motivation. Some students, no doubt, have made great progress; others may not have done so well. The wide variance in improvement is to be expected. Because reading skills are so exceedingly complex and interrelated, there is no one common beginning point for each individual student. If some students, however, did no more than solve their pace-breaking habits, the time and effort have been well spent.

Purpose, Practice, Review

We have said repeatedly that speed reading improvement evolves through purpose, practice, and review. If students' progress has not been as rewarding as they would have liked, they should review their goals for improving reading speed, reestablish a firm desire for progress, review and practice all exercises again, and restudy each skill discussed. If they follow these suggestions, students will soon discover personal improvement—even when reworking the exercises.

Reading Speeds

Students must remember that an efficient reader uses several reading speeds. Students are able to shift gears according to their backgrounds of experience, the difficulty of the material, the type of questions used to check their comprehension, and the basic reading purpose. It is difficult to say how many reading speeds are required for effective reading, but the following four reading rates should be more than adequate for meeting the requirements of students' assignments.

1. ***Skimming:*** The most rapid of all reading speeds used to locate a single item, name, or date in a text, or more importantly, the process of covering a chapter or many chapters to learn the author's central theme, main ideas, and supporting details.

2. ***Rapid Reading:*** The fastest rate at which every word in a selection can be read. The work pages of this book have been designed to improve this skill.

3. ***Study-Reading:*** The rate that requires slow, careful reading, and sometimes even rereading practice. This is the rate used for materials containing complex ideas, extraordinary vocabularies, or material in which every word, symbol, phrase, or even punctuation mark is important. Study-reading requires the art of careful, critical investigation; as such, it must be read more slowly than informational material of a general nature.

4. ***Recreational Reading:*** This is the rate used for personal or recreational pleasure. There is no determined drive to meet time or rate limits. The goal is pure pleasure. Of course, one may obtain an enormous amount of information using this rapid rate.

Students can further improve their reading rates regardless of the progress they've made so far. If they conscientiously utilize what they have already learned and practice regularly with all types of material, students will improve. To review suggestions made in previous lessons, we have listed them on the following page in capsule form.

SPEED READING REVIEW

1. Be sure you honestly want to improve your reading speed and are willing to work toward that goal.

2. Read much interesting material. This type of textual content will quickly erase those dreadful word-by-word habits. Without your personal application and practice, no speed reading course will succeed.

3. Practice daily. Set aside a time period each day for timed exercises. Read newspapers, newsmagazines, or anything of current interest. Force yourself to read more rapidly.

4. Improve your vocabulary. Never permit difficulties with word meaning to slow you down. Systematic planning provides great dividends.

5. Keep a daily record of your progress. It is better to read 500 wpm with 70 percent accuracy than 150 words with 100 percent accuracy.

6. Always predetermine your reading purpose. Know what your reading goals are, then read for those goals. Be persistent and realistic.

7. Skim daily. Look for word clues that tell you the writer is ready to list main ideas, basic principles, or summary statements.

8. Read and read much more. If you're going to be an expert reader, you must read often. So get into it, enjoy yourself, and good luck!

WARM-UP

INTERPRETATION EXERCISE

Time limit: 19 seconds

Directions: Check each item that can be pulled by people.

_____ 1. mountain		_____ 11. migraine headaches
_____ 2. string		_____ 12. pulmonary artery
_____ 3. winding river		_____ 13. drawstring
_____ 4. clouds		_____ 14. Pullman car
_____ 5. thoughts		_____ 15. jaded appetite
_____ 6. heavy burden		_____ 16. hot dog cart
_____ 7. hair		_____ 17. happy memories
_____ 8. two dalmatians		_____ 18. frivolous prose
_____ 9. tug-of-war		_____ 19. absentee landlord
_____ 10. wagon		_____ 20. pullover

Time _____   *Errors* _____   *Score* _____

PERCEPTION EXERCISE

Time limit: 24 seconds

Directions: Underline the same word as the key word.

Key Word

 1. secondary   secretary, secondary, ordinary, second
 2. universal   universal, untidy, unicycle, universe
 3. comical   cubical, comedy, comic, comical
 4. ozone   Ozark, zone, ozone, Oslo, orzo,
 5. kale   hale, kale, hail, kasbah, gale
 6. destroy   destiny, display, desolate, destroy
 7. medicine   medicine, medical, meddle, median
 8. fickle   pickle, middle, prickle, fickle, feeble
 9. calculator   calculus, calculate, calculator, carburetor
10. foam   moan, float, groan, fame, foot, foam
11. mystique   mist, mystery, mythical, mystique, mystify
12. hardwood   hardness, dogwood, hardly, hardwood, heartfelt
13. lactose   lactate, lactose, lacrosse, lacking, lactone
14. vanity   vanity, vain, vandal, vane, vanish
15. crane   cranberry, crab, crane, crack, craggy
16. ambulant   ambulance, ambulant, amulet, ambush, anhinga
17. proletariat   proletarize, proletarian, proletariat, proletary
18. midweekly   midweek, midwifery, midwinter, midweekly
19. heredity   here and away, hereditary, heredity, hereinafter
20. simulate   stimulate, similar, simulation, simulate, simplicity

Time _____   *Errors* _____   *Score* _____

COMPREHENSION EXERCISE   *Time limit: 34 seconds*

Directions: Underline the word or words that mean the same or about the same as the key word.

Key Word

1.	cabinet	wood, floor, organize the papers, cupboard
2.	elemental	last, school, children, chemistry, simple
3.	scribe	panic, run, write, project, illness
4.	cackle	laugh, cry, sing, shout, break
5.	pale	bucket, dry, distant, sale, lacking color
6.	mono	man, disaster, ending, alone, sad
7.	excise	join, take out, tax, exercise, join in
8.	verdict	judgment, summons, justice, ending, court
9.	window	air, beginning, opening, fastening, curtains
10.	however	never, before, into, just because, nevertheless
11.	jumpy	furry, edgy, higher, kangaroo, beans
12.	soaked	rainy, drenched, inside, downpour, drip
13.	eventually	to be, happening, at the start, finally, before
14.	gross	green, effervescent, total, grip, grabby
15.	screen	protect, scream, vanilla, able, loud noise
16.	verily	efficiently, sloppily, with force, carefully, truly
17.	magnificence	extremely happy, enlarge, greatness, burned
18.	hyper	happy, small, overexcited, sleepy, late
19.	coat	fur, under, bear, keep, rack, animal
20.	scruples	food, joke, millennium, ethics, dreamlike

Time _____   *Errors* _____   *Score* _____

STORY I

Some people make a living by tasting and smelling. Highly trained professionals, known as sensory analysts, help manufacturers ensure quality control, develop new products, and respond to consumer complaints. These much sought-after "detectives" seek out the *top-notes*, which are the first aromas and tastes that are perceived by the senses, and the *off-notes*, which are aromas and tastes that don't belong in the product, and everything in between. Sensory analysts work for breweries, pasta makers, confectioners, wineries, and perfumeries, among other corporations. For example, if a cola company decided to compare its product with the leading cola on the market, a sensory analyst might be employed. He or she would likely provide computerized data on the physical properties (color, texture, and effervescence) as well as the chemical properties (aroma and basic taste).

A sensory analyst must be able to identify the basic tastes: sweet, sour, bitter, and salty. (Many beginners confuse bitter and sour; lemon has a sour taste, while black coffee has a bitter taste.) And a good sensory analyst can easily identify a phenolic compound by its resin odor—like that of bandage tape, or a "hospital" smell. Phenolic compounds are used in inks and packaging, and too much resin odor can detract from a product or even ruin it. In order to function effectively in their work, sensory analysts wear no perfume, cologne, body lotion, or hair spray. Furthermore, they neither eat nor drink for at least 30 minutes before rating a product.

1. Sensory analysts can be effectively employed by (a) wine makers, (b) book makers, (c) soda companies, (d) both a and c.

2. The first aromas and tastes that are perceived by the senses are called (a) high-notes, (b) low-notes, (c) top-notes, (d) sharps.

3. People who work with their senses of taste and smell are called (a) food tasters, (b) sensory analysts, (c) beefeaters, (d) anteaters.

4. They might give the manufacturer advice on (a) consumer complaints, (b) pricing, (c) location, (d) health foods.

5. Off-notes are aromas and tastes that (a) disappear, (b) smell and taste like tree bark, (c) are flat, (d) don't belong in the product.

6. The taste of lemon is (a) bitter, (b) sweet, (c) salty, (d) sour.

7. The odor from bandage tape probably comes from a (a) phenolic compound, (b) Hyannis Port compound, (c) phenethyl compound, (d) none of these.

8. During work hours, sensory analysts don't wear (a) lotion, (b) cologne, (c) hair spray, (d) a, b, and c.

9. They avoid food and drink for at least (a) 10 minutes, (b) 15 minutes, (c) 30 minutes, (d) one hour.

10. The four basic tastes are sweet, sour, salty, and (a) sugary, (b) flat, (c) bitter, (d) oily.

STORY II

It mysteriously hovers over the water like gauze, forming a misty, transparent barrier. And you can even touch it—it's dry and cold. If you've never seen it before, you might mistake it for fog. Meteorologists call it sea smoke, but it's also known as steam fog, Arctic frost smoke, and vapor. The appearance of sea smoke can astound the uninitiated. Its confluence of temperatures can create three-inch icicles on a man's beard. Sea smoke can also freeze into layers heavy enough to make a boat list.

Scientists tell us that this phenomenon originates with winter air that blows for hundreds of miles across the evergreen forests of subarctic lands and the snowy, treeless plains of Arctic regions. When this air reaches a warmer coastal region, it meets with a sheet of moist air just above the water. This air is only slightly warmer than the air above it. When the cold, foreign air moves across the coastal pocket, the extreme temperatures mix. Immediately, the moisture condenses as the warmer air lifts, creating an earthbound cloud as fine as mist. The scientific explanation for sea smoke is a result of moisture in an air mass reaching its saturation point. Seawater provides a welcoming environment for these conditions since it absorbs and releases heat slowly. Coastal regions that boast varied temperatures from season to season are the most likely to host sea smoke.

1. Sea smoke is compared to a (a) barn, (b) wizard, (c) transparent barrier, (d) smoke.

2. We can infer that the vision of sea smoke is (a) eerie, (b) warm, (c) bright, (d) opaque.

3. If you've never seen sea smoke, you might think that it is (a) a cloud, (b) fog, (c) rain, (d) snow.

4. Another name for sea smoke is (a) sea wind, (b) sea breeze, (c) Arctic frost smoke, (d) fog.

5. Sea smoke has been known to create icicles on (a) clouds, (b) hair, (c) rain, (d) itself.

6. When invading air falls across a warmer moist sheet of air, the moist air (a) causes thunder, (b) does nothing, (c) condenses, (d) both a and c.

7. Sea smoke is as fine as (a) mist, (b) flour, (c) oil, (d) smoke.

8. Sea smoke is a result of moisture reaching its (a) height, (b) density, (c) critical mass, (d) saturation point.

9. Vapor is attracted to (a) seawater, (b) people, (c) freshwater, (d) mountains.

10. Seawater absorbs and releases heat (a) quickly, (b) slowly, (c) never, (d) rarely.

GWPM _____ *(times) Avg. Comp.* _____ *(equals) EWPM* _____

Appendix

Figure 1

Daily Record of *Interpretation* Skills

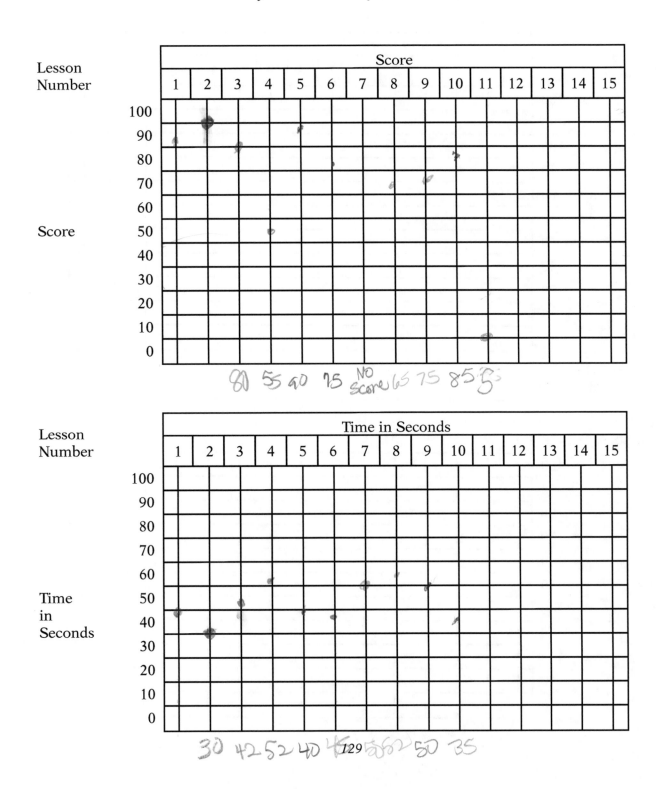

Figure 2

Daily Record of *Perception* Skills

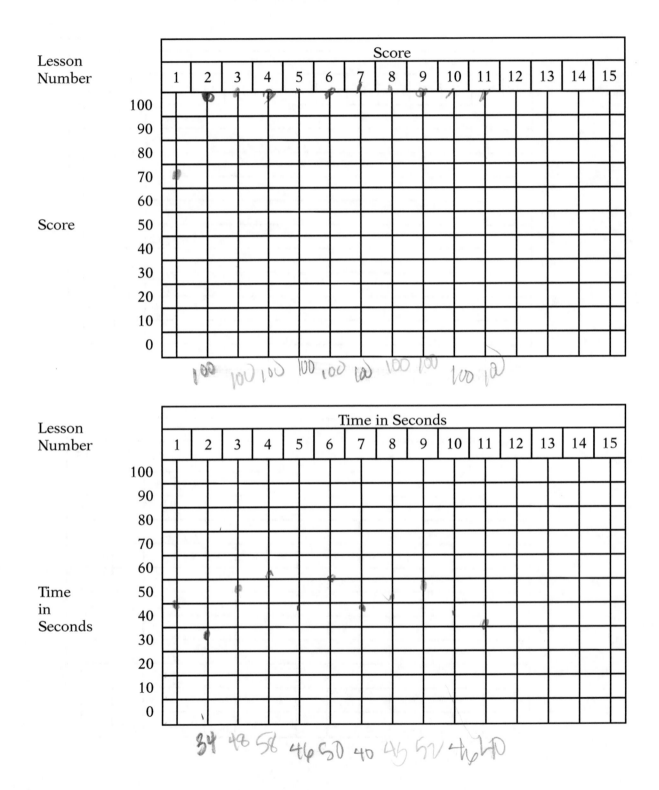

Figure 3

Daily Record of *Comprehension* Skills

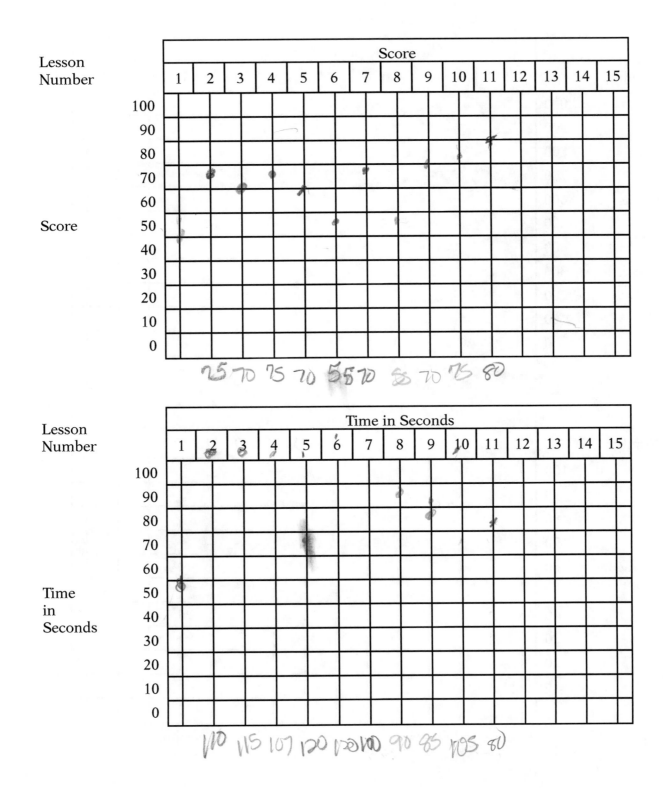

Figure 4

Daily Rate and Comprehension Chart

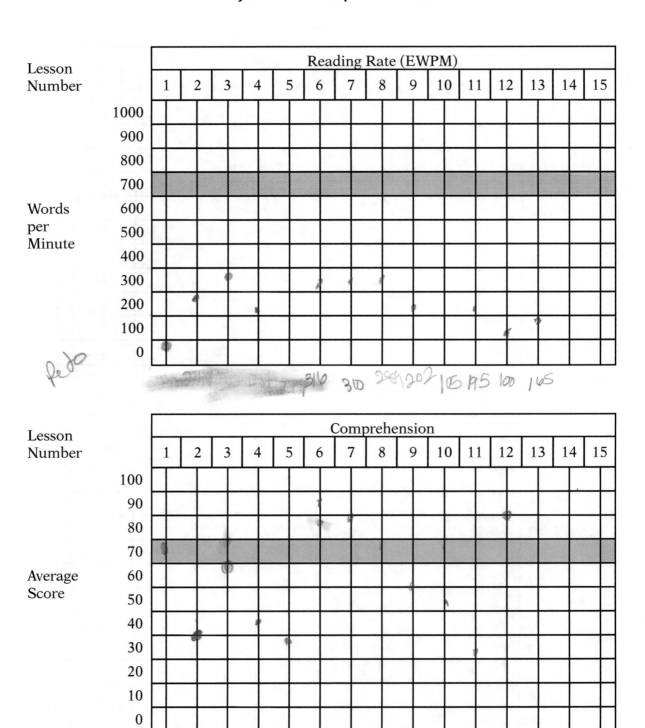

Scores of both daily stories are averaged for this graph.

Table 1

Speed Reading Achievement Chart

Lesson Number	Gross Words per Minute	x	Average Comprehension Score	=	Effective Words per Minute (drop off last two digits)
1 (pretest)	55		70		38.5
2	244		40		97.6
3	362		60		217
4	204		45		93
5	274		35		95
6	372		85		316
7	388		80		310
8	386		75		289
9	404		50		202
10	434		45		195
11	336		30		100
12	206		80		165
13					
14					
15 (posttest)					

Percent of Improvement: _____%

Pretest score subtracted from posttest score, multiplied by 100, divided by the pretest score, equals the percent of improvement for the course.

We want to hear from you! Your valuable comments and suggestions will help us meet your current and future classroom needs.

Your name_____Date_____

School name_____Phone_____

School address_____

Grade level taught_____Subject area(s) taught_____Average class size_____

Where did you purchase this publication?_____

Was your salesperson knowledgeable about this product?   Yes_____   No_____

What monies were used to purchase this product?

_____School supplemental budget   _____Federal/state funding   _____Personal

Please "grade" this Walch publication according to the following criteria:

Quality of service you received when purchasing .... A	B	C	D	F
Ease of use.. A	B	C	D	F
Quality of content.. A	B	C	D	F
Page layout .... A	B	C	D	F
Organization of material .... A	B	C	D	F
Suitability for grade level .... A	B	C	D	F
Instructional value... A	B	C	D	F

COMMENTS:_____

_____

What specific supplemental materials would help you meet your current—or future—instructional needs?

_____

Have you used other Walch publications? If so, which ones?_____

May we use your comments in upcoming communications?   _____Yes   _____No

Please **FAX** this completed form to **207-772-3105**, or mail it to:

Product Development, J.Weston Walch, Publisher, P.O. Box 658, Portland, ME 04104-0658

We will send you a **FREE GIFT** as our way of thanking you for your feedback. **THANK YOU!**